The Complete Guide to the Sheffield and South Yorkshire Navigation

Christine Richardson and John Lower

*On your Anniversary
with lots of love
from
Narendra and Maria*

The Hallamshire Press

A Richlow Guide

Text © 1995 Interleaf Productions Limited
Photographs and Maps © 1995 John Lower and Christine Richardson

Published by The Hallamshire Press
The Hallamshire Press is an imprint of
Interleaf Productions Limited
Exchange Works
Sidney Street
Sheffield SI 3QF
England

Typeset by Interleaf Productions Limited
Printed in Singapore by
Saik Wah Press Pte Ltd

British Library Cataloguing in Publication Data

Richardson, Christine
    Complete Guide to the Sheffield and
    South Yorkshire Navigation
    I. Title II. Lower, John
    386.48094282

ISBN 1-874718-07-5

Contents

Acknowledgements

We wish to thank the many people who have helped with information for this guide, and especially Richard Mercer and his staff (British Waterways), Phil Jervis (Rotherham Metropolitan Borough Council), Malcolm Fielding (Inland Waterways Association), and Philip Scowcroft (Railway and Canal Historical Society).

Cover photograph: Sprotbrough

Key to Maps

CP = Car Park
FC = Fish & Chip Shop
G   = Garage (Fuel)
GS = General Store
LB = Letter Box
PH = Public House
PO = Post Office
T   = Telephone
LC = Level crossing
RD = Rubbish Disposal
SS = Sanitary Station
W   = Water Point
Sh = Shower
M   = Moorings

▬▬▬ Navigable Waterway

– – – Towpath

······· Towpath to be constructed

◪ Lift-bridge

▯ Swing-bridge (red spot indicates position of control panel)

╫─■─╫ Railway and Station

╫─■─╫ South Yorkshire Supertram and Station

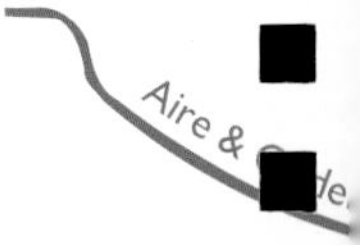

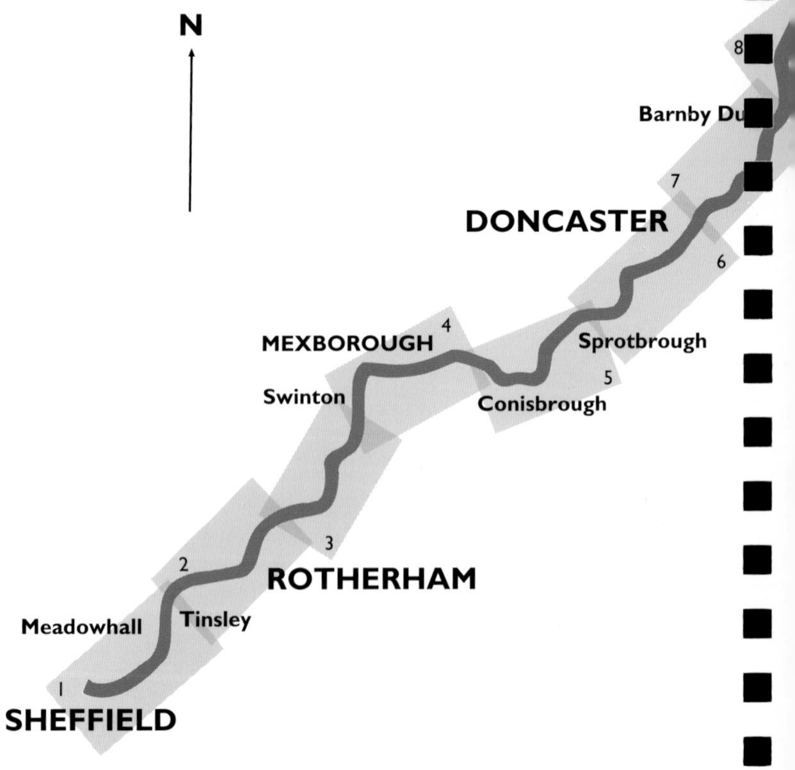

N

Aire & Calde...

8

Barnby Du...

7

DONCASTER

6

MEXBOROUGH 4   Sprotbrough

Swinton   5

Conisbrough

3

2   **ROTHERHAM**

Meadowhall Tinsley

1

SHEFFIELD

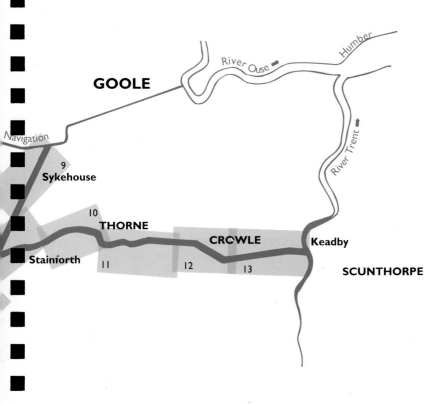

Distances (in miles)

Sheffield Basin

6½	Rotherham									
11	4½	Kilnhurst								
13	6½	2	Mexborough							
18	11½	7	5	Sprotbrough						
21½	15	10½	8½	3½	Doncaster New Moorings					
28	21½	17	15	10	6½	Bramwith Junction				
33	26½	22	20	15	11½	5	Thorne			
39½	33	28½	26½	21½	18	11½	6½	Crowle Station		
43	36½	32	30	25	21½	15	10	3½	Keadby	

Main Line

Bramwith Junction

1¾	Kirkhouse Green Bridge		
3½	1¾	Sykehouse Lock	
5½	3¾	2	Southfield Junction

New Junction Canal

5

Sailing keel passing through Keadby Lock, circa 1920
Reproduced by kind permission of Lincolnshire County Council, Recreational Services

Introduction

This guide covers the 49 miles of the Sheffield & South Yorkshire Navigation, via Sheffield, Rotherham, Doncaster, Thorne and Keadby.

It contains practical information for walkers, road visitors, cyclists, anglers and boaters. Also included are interesting facts about what can be seen today, the Navigation's history, and the wildlife and plants. A section on boat access via the River Trent is on pages 90-91.

The authors are local enthusiasts who, over a number of years, have explored the Navigation by foot and by boat. They have supplied photographs for waterways calendars, written various books on the subject, and are regular contributors to national magazines.

Care should always be taken at deep water locations such as locks and river wharfs. Diving and swimming are not allowed in the SSYN — there are underwater sluices and machinery, and passing boats create invisible currents.

Not all of the towpath is public right-of-way; where this is so British Waterways allow use, but do not guarantee good conditions.

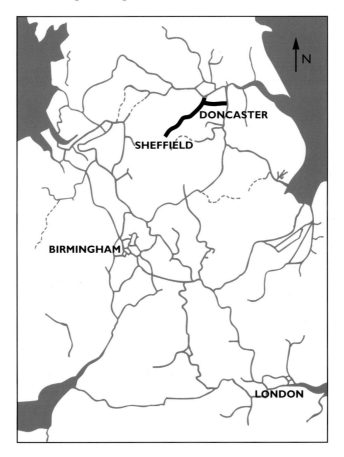

Brief Description

The Sheffield & South Yorkshire Navigation is a collective name for four waterways, namely the Sheffield & Tinsley Canal, the River Don, the New Junction Canal, and the Stainforth & Keadby Canal.

Although they are now known by one title, each of the four waterways has a varied history, and as a result the Navigation is a diverse mixture. Some locks are old and operated manually; others are cavernous modern structures, electrically powered. Moveable bridges — some lift, others swing; one retracts — are numerous on the eastern lengths.

In addition, the areas through which the Navigation passes could not be more dissimilar: from Sheffield city centre with its restored canal basin, through Rotherham's improved town landscape, between tree-lined river banks, to the vast open acreage of the flat lands near the River Trent. In Sheffield and Rotherham, signs of the Navigation's industrial heritage can still be found — cranes, wharfs, warehouses. Near Thorne, wild deer sometimes fall into the canal and there is a ramp to aid their escape.

The river sections of the SSYN can be unpredictable. After heavy prolonged rain, the water level rises and the flow is very fast. On the man-made canals the environment remains static.

Walking

On the canals the towpath is good, but there are places on the River Don where there is no path. However, all the local councils and British Waterways are working to improve the situation and in the future the Trans Pennine Trail will use some of the riverside lengths. Where walkable, the towpath is shown on the maps.

Navigation

The whole of the SSYN is navigable; the locks are wide but some are less than 65 feet long. The two access points are from the Aire & Calder Navigation at Goole, and from the tidal River Trent at Keadby. Trail-boats may use various slipways. Navigational information is on pages 20-21.

Angling

The major fisheries are on the New Junction Canal and the Stainforth & Keadby Canal. The standard is high and international matches are held there. Details of the clubs involved and the fish available are on page 19.

Cycling

Towpaths on the Sheffield and Rotherham lengths are being restored to cycleway standards. See page 18.

Walkers passing Yorkshire Rose Marina, Mexborough

History

In other areas, rivers were superseded by canals as navigable waterways, but in the north-east they formed the basis of the whole network. The River Don is the central strand of the SSYN, with its three associated canals built as extensions to it. The Stainforth & Keadby Canal provided an outlet to the Trent that was more efficient than the Don's route to the River Ouse. The Sheffield & Tinsley Canal took boats to the city centre. The New Junction Canal was a link to the thriving Aire & Calder Navigation.

A fourth canal, the Dearne & Dove, was part of the SSYN but it is unnavigable now. Perhaps it will regain its place when its energetic restoration volunteers are successful.

Early Developments

The River Don has been navigable to Doncaster for many centuries, although its lower reaches followed a different route from that known today. The river had a delta-like confluence with the Trent and the Ouse, flowing through undrained marshlands. By the 1700s Thorne, on one of these branches, had developed into a thriving port and boat-building centre.

The land flooded by the Don was too valuable to remain unused, and in 1626 King Charles I made an agreement with the Dutch engineer Vermuyden to drain the vast marshy area. Eventually the Don was forced into one artificial channel, flowing into the Ouse at Goole. This is why the lower reaches of the Don are straight and why its name in that area changes to the Dutch River. Vermuyden's drainage works were extensive and not always popular, as diverted waters caused problems elsewhere. There were riots in Fishlake and Sykehouse.

Navigation in the confined Don (Dutch River) was never easy; at high-flow times it was dangerous. Nevertheless, it was the major waterway of south Yorkshire, and over the centuries many improvements were proposed to make it navigable nearer to Sheffield.

Don Navigation Company

By 1721 Sheffield's trade was suffering from a lack of transport. Each year 12,000 tons of hardware left the city for Hull, and the Cutlers' Company wanted this carried on the Don. Eventually an Act of Parliament was obtained, and in 1733 a new body was formed to manage the river — the Company of Proprietors of the Navigation of the River Dun (the company always used the old name Dun instead of Don).

By 1740 the river was navigable to Rotherham. However, the lower reaches were still difficult: in dry seasons there was only 8–9 inches of water depth and boats were stuck for days in the shallows. This was no good for trade. Many improvements were made — locks and artificial cuts — and Thorne became the primary transhipment point between river and coastal vessels. Boats could reach Tinsley, on the outskirts of Sheffield, by 1751 and that has remained the Don's head of navigation.

The river and the company thrived. Thorne became a busy port, with a popular paddle-steamer service to Goole and Hull. By 1823 the Don Navigation Company was making a major contribution to transport in south Yorkshire.

Three Canals

The canal age started to boom in the 1770s, and a radical solution was proposed to bypass the Don's lower reaches — a canal outlet to the River Trent. Completed in 1802 by a separate company, the Stainforth & Keadby Canal was of great benefit to the Don Navigation, although some traffic continued to use the old route, especially to Thorne's river port.

In 1793 the Don Navigation Company sponsored a canal from its waterway at Swinton to the rich Barnsley coalfield — the Dearne & Dove. At the same time, there were moves for a canal to Sheffield from the Don's head of navigation at Tinsley. The existing road was crowded because the steel companies had rapidly increased weapons production for the Napoleonic Wars. An Act of Parliament was obtained in 1815. Work progressed quickly and the grand opening in Sheffield Basin was on 22nd February 1819, attended by nearly 60,000 people. The Sheffield & Tinsley Canal was built and owned by a separate company, but it — and the Stainforth & Keadby, and the Dearne & Dove — eventually came under the control of the powerful Don Navigation Company.

The Railway Years

Over the years, the Don Navigation had been refined and improved; as a result, when the railway age began, the company was well able to meet the challenge. Even so, rather than compete, it was decided to merge with rail companies while shareholders would still receive a good price. In 1850 the Don Navigation Company — together with the canals it had acquired — amalgamated with the South Yorkshire, Doncaster & Goole Railway to form the South Yorkshire Railway & River Don Company: a combined rail-waterway transport system.

Edith T *leaving Sheffield Basin
after delivering a cargo of grain,
mid 1950 s*
Waterways Archives

*In the late 1960s, 100-ton
capacity craft deliver coal to
Doncaster Power Station*
Waterways Archives

This started a period of mergers, the outcome of which was the dissolution of the previous companies in 1874 when everything — river, canals, railways — was transferred to the MSLR (Manchester, Sheffield & Lincolnshire Railway). Within the new organisation, water was less important than rail and the result was the usual loss of traffic. But because of the nearby coalfields, and the ability to carry large vessels, the Navigation did not close like the narrow canals of other areas.

Sheffield & South Yorkshire Navigation

The Navigation's current name is one borrowed from the past. In the late 1880s public opinion thought the local waterways were not being efficiently operated, and if Manchester could have a new ship canal then South Yorkshire should also have modern waterways. A new company was formed to buy the old Don Navigation's collection of waterways from the MSLR, and it was called the Sheffield & South Yorkshire Navigation Company. Commercially the venture was quite successful, but the administration was confused. In 1898 almost one million tons was carried, but profits fell from £36,000 in 1888 to £24,000 in 1905. Some improvements were made, but it could never raise the money for enlargement plans, although Sheffield Basin was modernised.

New Junction Canal

A long-cherished dream of the original Don Navigation Company had been a link to the thriving and ambitious Aire & Calder Navigation. In 1891 such a scheme was approved as a joint venture of the Aire & Calder and the SSYN. The main reason for its construction was to allow the efficient system of compartment boats already working on the A&C access to the Don and its adjacent coalfields.

Completed in 1905, it is said to be the last new canal built in England. It was not the success it might have been; certainly the trade uncertainties caused by the First World War did not help.

Twentieth Century

Between the two World Wars, improvements continued but times were difficult. Many boats had been requisitioned by the Admiralty and had sunk on war service, continental trade patterns changed, costs rose, and manpower was unavailable. But the Humber keels continued to make their way up to Sheffield and the boatmen and their families were still a distinct part of society. In 1933 the SSYN waterways carried 628,391 tons of various cargoes.

Just before the Second World War, the old lock at Stainforth between the canal and the river was closed, ending centuries of trade on the Dutch River (Don) because Thorne's old river port had continued to operate, even when most of the traffic used the Stainforth & Keadby Canal. In 1940 the Sheffield blitz damaged Tinsley Locks.

In the 1950s control of the waterways passed to the Docks & Inland Waterways Executive. Loading staithes were built for power stations and in 1951 the SSYN carried over one million tons for the first time. A new warehouse complex was built at Rotherham in the 1960s and this became the head of commercial operations; the last cargo into Sheffield Basin was a load of maize in December 1970.

Modernisation in the 1980s

This is a tale of missed opportunities. As early as 1920 the Government was turning down schemes to improve the commercial use of the Navigation. Throughout the 1960s and 1970s local councils and British Waterways sought Government funding. After many delays a scheme was approved in 1978 — at a cost of £10m, the SSYN was to be rebuilt to take single 700-ton barges or push-tow units totalling 420 tons as far upstream as Rotherham. An area near Aldwarke lock was to become 'Rotherport', a large road-rail-water interchange to link with Europe via Hull. The main route was along the New Junction Canal; the waterway to Keadby was not included.

The work was done speedily, but the decades of delay, and the financial burdens imposed by the Government, meant that the scheme was completed in the depth of a recession. It was all too late. By 1985 cargo totals had fallen drastically short of expectations. The converted garage/wharf/warehouse at Parkgate (Rotherham) is the sorry remnant of the 'Rotherport' dreams.

Some commercial carrying still takes place, and anti-road pressures may see this increase. British Waterways is continually seeking new contracts.

Boats of the SSYN

Keels

The most numerous vessels were sailing barges called 'keels'. Built for the Navigation's dimensions, they were known as 'Sheffield size', 61 feet by 15 feet 6 inches. Their main source of cargo was Hull docks, so the SSYN's craft had to use the mighty waters of the Humber as well as canals. They could sail between Hull and Keadby, but were often towed by steam-tugs, as many as eight at a time.

Between Keadby and Mexborough, many craft sailed because that was the cheapest form of propulsion. Upstream of Mexborough, sailing was difficult because the mast had to be lowered to pass under the many fixed bridges. So they left their sails at Mexborough Lock and hired a horse and handler known as a 'horse-marine' to tow them further upstream. Mexborough was the major base of horse-marines, but there were others at Attercliffe, Rotherham, Kilnhurst, Swinton, Stainforth, Thorne and Keadby.

The decline of the horse-marines started in 1931 when diesel tugs began towing keels. By 1939 the tugs were not needed because many keels had engines and they towed their powerless sisters. In the late 1940s almost all craft were diesel-engined and the graceful square sails were no longer seen across the flat landscape.

Tom Puddings

The keels brought cargoes to and from Hull, but the internal canal coal trade was carried in compartment boats, strung together to form a 'train' propelled by one tug. They were known as 'Tom Puddings' and thirty boats could be linked in one long line. Developed on the neighbouring Aire & Calder Navigation in the 1860s, they were successful for a hundred years. At Goole the individual boats were lifted up a tower and tipped over — their coal cascading down into a sea-going ship moored below. Only one Tom Pudding hoist has

survived; a film of it in operation can be viewed at the adjacent Sobriety Centre in Goole.

A modern system now operates with push-pull tugs each propelling three large linked 'pans'. Coal is taken to Ferrybridge Power Station on the Aire & Calder Navigation, but they operate on the SSYN when a good coal source can be found.

Ferries, Aquabuses and Packet-Boats

Aquabuses. By 1840 the new railway system had reached Swinton, but not Doncaster, so a boat service was started to fill the gap. Its 'aquabuses' were 66 feet long and the speed and fares compared well with the rival road coaches — 10mph; fore-cabin 9d, best cabin 1s. They ran to a regular timetable, called at Conisbrough and Sprotbrough, and were soon carrying 1,456 passengers a week. They became redundant in 1849 when the South Yorkshire Railway reached Doncaster.

Ferries. From early centuries small boats have ferried passengers across the Don Navigation. Some lasted well into the 20th century but all have now ceased — Bramwith, Doncaster, Newton, Sprotbrough, Conisbrough. At Mexborough an inscribed ferry post has survived (see pages 15 and 48).

Packet-boats. Up to 1856 a horse-drawn packet-boat took passengers between Thorne and Keadby, linking with the steam-packets on the River Trent Hull–Gainsborough service.

In the mid-1950s, Junior T *has difficulty passing empty beneath Bacon Lane Bridge, Sheffield—the most restrictive on the navigation.*
R. Frost

Interesting Features to Look For Along the Navigation

Swing-Bridges and Lift-Bridges

These are moveable to allow boats to pass through otherwise low bridges. The Stainforth & Keadby Canal has many swing-bridges; the New Junction Canal has both varieties. They are usually operated by boat crews.

Rope Grooves

The old keels could not sail very well upstream of Mexborough because of all the fixed bridges, so they were pulled by horse up to Sheffield. The tow-rope between a horse and a boat was quite long. When a boat-horse emerged from under a bridge and regained the towpath, the boat was some way behind and was still passing under the bridge. Therefore the tow-rope was at an angle and rubbed against the edge of the bridge and, many boats later, wore grooves in the brickwork. Bridge No. 9 at Sheffield has rope grooves in the metal guards fixed to protect it.

Stop-Grooves

On the canals where the channel is narrower than elsewhere — often under bridges or at the end of aqueducts — there may be a vertical groove in the stone or brickwork on both banks, at the waterline. If the canal is leaking, or a length has to be drained for maintenance work, then the required section can be dammed off by slotting planks into these grooves: under Bridge 9 in Sheffield for example.

Aqueducts

These are structures carrying waterways over other features. The New Junction Canal has aqueducts over the rivers Don and Went. The Sheffield & Tinsley Canal has an aqueduct over a busy road.

Tide Locks

Keadby Lock is the link between a canal and a tidal river. Such locks often have four sets of gates instead of the usual two. Normally, the water level in the canal at Keadby is higher than it is in the river, and gates 1 and 2 are used. However, when the tidal river rises to be higher than the canal the lock is still operational by using gates 3 and 4 (see diagram opposite).

Boats

Sobriety and *Eden* are boats of the Sobriety Project, a charity supplying residential trips for school groups and people with special needs. *Sobriety* is a motorised Humber keel, built in 1910 and working under sail until the 1940s. *Eden* is a Leeds & Liverpool Canal motor barge built in 1936.

Spider is a wide-beam craft based at Eastwood Lock, which takes groups on educational and residential trips: a non-profit making community venture.

Wyre Lady is owned by Alan Oliver Cruises Ltd, and is sometimes moored near Sprotbrough Lock. She was launched 1938 on the Clyde. During World War II she took supplies to the liners *Queen Mary* and *Queen Elizabeth* when they were troopships, and also worked on the Forth & Clyde Canal, and the rivers Wyre and Severn. She now operates as the Sprotbrough water-bus on summer Sundays and Bank Holidays, and does party cruises.

Further information on cargo carrying craft is on page 55.

British Waterways

BW facilities for boaters are mooring points above and below locks, as boats must stop to open the gates if no lock-keeper is on duty; and at strategic sites there are rubbish bins, toilet disposal points, and taps for filling drinking water tanks. Most are kept locked and crews open them with a special BW (Watermate) key. Long-term and visitor moorings are also provided. Most of the navigable canals in Britain belong to the state-owned British Waterways. They are also responsible for navigational matters on some rivers otherwise administered by the National Rivers Authority.

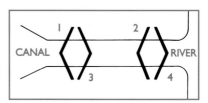

1. Bridge name plate; 2. Lock gate capstan;
3. Winding bollard; 4. Navigation company notice

Two faces of the flood level and ferry stone at Mexborough

New Junction Canal milepost

Sheffield & Tinsley milepost

Boats regularly seen on the Navigation

Walking: General

Of the four waterways that form the SSYN, the three canals have complete towpaths but the Don Navigation, as a canalised river, is not walkable throughout. However, Rotherham and Doncaster Councils, and British Waterways, are planning through-paths for the future. The current situation is available from British Waterways' Doncaster office (page 94).

Sheffield & Tinsley Canal and Don Navigation

With the completion of a new towpath section in Rotherham in early 1995, there will be a good-quality path between Sheffield and Rotherham with rail stations easily accessible at both ends. Also Sheffield Supertram provides return transport from Tinsley Locks.

Don Navigation and Stainforth & Keadby Canal

The SSYN is well served by rail: the nine stations are fully listed on page 93. As a result, many walks can be planned with public return transport available.

New Junction Canal and Stainforth & Keadby Canal

The land between these two waterways is very low lying and consequently it can be wet underfoot. The New Junction Canal is not served by rail.

Five Weirs Walk, Sheffield

The River Don runs parallel to the SSYN from the centre of Sheffield to Meadowhall, nearly 5 miles. The Five Weirs Walk (and cycleway) is being formed along this length, its name a reference to the weirs built when Sheffield's industries used the river. Now the water quality in the river is improving, and there has been an improvement in fish stocks and wildlife, including kingfishers, herons, fig trees, trout and coarse fish. The walk is a traffic-free corridor through the city and care has been taken to ensure people with disabilities can use the paths. A bridge at Meadowhall is planned to give access to the SSYN so that the canal towpath and the Five Weirs Walk along the River Don will form a ten-mile round route. A walk leaflet is available from Sheffield Tourist Information (see page 94).

Trans Pennine Trail

This system of paths is being developed and it will use sections of the SSYN.

Walks Leaflets

Available from Doncaster Tourist Information (page 94) are leaflets on walks in the Thorne area.

A Round Walk from Fishlake: three circular walks from 5 to 10 miles.
Fishlake Heritage Trail: a circular walk, 5.5 miles. This is a lovely and historic village, accessible from the SSYN via the bridge at Stainforth.
Thorne Round Walk: three circular walks, from 3.5 miles to 11.5 miles.
The Doncastrian Way: a 33-mile circular walk, divided into five sections. Includes Barnby Dun to Doncaster, and Sprotbrough to Doncaster.

Cycling

A permit is required to cycle on British Waterways towpaths, available from BW's Newark office (see page 94). There is no charge for the permit. When riding on the towpath, consideration is to be shown to other users.

By the summer of 1995 there will be a cycle-standard towpath between Sheffield Basin (Victoria Quays) and Rotherham Lock (Maps 1 and 2).

Sections of the towpaths along the New Junction Canal and the Stainforth & Keadby Canal are also usable. However, these parts of the SSYN are a major fishery of National Championships standard, and use of the towpath by anglers should be taken into account in the fishing season.

As shown on the maps, there is no continuous towpath along the SSYN. British Waterways and the local councils are planning to increase the paths in Rotherham and Doncaster, and the Trans Pennine Trail will use sections of the River Don's banks.

At the time of writing, cycles are not allowed on Sheffield's Supertram system.

● A national cycle information pack is available, £5 post paid, from British Waterways, Customer Services Dept, Willow Grange, Church Road, Watford WD1 3QA.

Angling

A National Rivers Authority rod licence is required before fishing freshwater in England and Wales; it is available from most fishing tackle shops and Post Offices. However, the holder of a rod licence must still obtain the permission of the owner or tenant of the fishing rights.

The rights on the whole of the SSYN are licensed to angling clubs who control the day-to-day fishing on their length of waterway. These clubs usually make their waters available to non-members by day-permits, often sold on the towpath by a patrolling bailiff. Prices of day-permits vary from 75p to £2 or so. If day-permits are not available, signs at bridges will normally state that fishing is for members only.

Fishing is from the towpath and is not encouraged from boats as this may cause navigational hazards. Boats have priority at recognised mooring sites and no fishing at all may take place from lock landings, water points and waste disposal points. Also please remember that walkers and cyclists are entitled to use the towpath and must not be obstructed by fishing tackle. The British Waterways' code of practice for anglers is available from any BW office (see page 94).

Disabled Anglers

Wiseman's Bridge (Map 12) over a parallel drainage ditch gives ramped access to the canal towpath. A car park is by the bridge.

Crowle Wharf (Map 12) has ramped access and a wheelchair-secure fishing platform.

Sheffield & Tinsley Canal

First-class canal fishery. Roach, perch, carp, gudgeon.

River Don (Tinsley to Sprotbrough)

Poorer water quality means fishing is patchy: some areas satisfactory, others poor. Roach, perch, some carp.

River Don (downstream of Sprotbrough), New Junction Canal, Stainforth & Keadby Canal

Very good fishing, heavily used for contests, e.g. the 1994 National Championships. Roach, chub, gudgeon, bream.

Angling Clubs

Sheffield & Tinsley Canal

Sheffield Basin to Cadman St. No fishing.

The rest of the canal is divided into many lengths, the rights on each belonging to various clubs. Details often change; the latest information is available from British Waterways (Newark) (see page 94).

Don Navigation

Upstream of Mexborough. Details from British Waterways (Newark) (see page 94).

Mexborough Top Lock – Sprotbrough. Rotherham & District UAF. Mr B. Turner, 91 Cherrytree St, Elsecar, Barnsley. Tel: 01226 746297.

Sprotbrough – Long Sandall Rail Bridge. Doncaster & District AA. Mr M. Tate, 28 Holmescarr Rd, Rossington, Doncaster DN11 0QF. Tel: 01302 865482.

Long Sandall Rail Bridge – Old Bridge, Kirk Sandall. Pilkington AC. Mr J. Butterley, Pilkington Rec. Club, Old Kirk Sandall, Doncaster DN3 1HW.

Old Bridge, Kirk Sandall – Barnby Dun Bridge. Barnby Dun Social AC. Mr W. Salter, 1 Greengates, High St, Barnby Dun, Doncaster DN3 1DU. Tel: 01302 886024.

Barnby Dun Bridge – Bramwith Junction. Doncaster & District AA. As above.

New Junction Canal

The whole canal. Doncaster & District AA. As above.

Stainforth & Keadby Canal

Bramwith Lock – Stainforth Bridge. Stainforth Town Council. Mrs C. Taylor, Travellers Rest Farm, Norton, Doncaster DN6 9HF.

Dunston Hill Bridge – Maud's Bridge. Thorne Town Council. Mr E. McGarry, Thorne Town Council, Assembly Rooms, Fieldside, Thorne, Doncaster DN8 4AE.

Maud's Bridge – Keadby Basin. Stainforth & Keadby Joint Angling Committee. Mr J. Cunliffe, 13 Wesley Rd, Kiveton Park, Sheffield S31 8RJ. Tel: 01909 772587.

Boating on the SSYN

General Comments

The SSYN consists of three canals and one river navigation, with a necessarily varied pattern of lock and bridge types. However, they are all very wide waterways, although some locks are less than 65 feet long (see below).

Access is from the Aire & Calder Navigation at Southfields Junction, and from the River Trent via Keadby Lock, operation of which is tide-dependent.

With the exception of the lock and two movable bridges at Keadby, all locks and swing- or lift-bridges can be operated by boat crews.

With the exception of the Sheffield & Tinsley Canal, the waterways of the SSYN are capable of carrying commercial craft. The amount of such traffic varies, and is sometimes scarce, but the possibility of meeting large vessels should always be borne in mind.

SSYN Waterways

Stainforth & Keadby Canal	13 miles
New Junction Canal	5 miles
Don Navigation	25 miles
Sheffield & Tinsley Canal	4 miles

Maximum Dimensions (in feet)

	Length	Beam	Draught	Airdraught
Keadby Lock	77	21		
Keadby – Bramwith Jnc	61‡	17‡	7	10
New Junction Canal	200	20	8	11
Bramwith Jnc –				
Rotherham	200	20	8	11
Rotherham – Sheffield	61	15‡	4	9‡

‡ Thorne Lock
‡ Bacon Lane Bridge

Keys Required

A British Waterways' Sanitary Station (Watermate) key is essential to operate moveable bridges, powered locks when the keepers are absent, and the top paddles on the manual locks.

This system is being installed in early 1995 to supersede the old method that required a special key obtainable from Long Sandall and Eastwood locks. If unsure, check with BW's Doncaster office (see page 94).

A standard windlass is also required for unpowered locks.

Locks

Some locks are manned by BW staff and may be called on Marine Band radio, Channel 74.

The keepers' duty hours are kept under review, but they are usually present midweek because the SSYN is a commercial waterway.

In the keepers' absence, the locks are crew-operated. If unsure about using such large locks, ask the Long Sandall lock-keeper for advice when passing through.

Some power-operated locks have red/green traffic lights; only Thorne has amber as on the Trent. There is no official code of usage.

Stainforth & Keadby Canal

Keadby lock is *always* operated by the BW keeper; the hours are on page 91. For Thorne Lock, see the maximum dimensions table above.

New Junction Canal and the Don Navigation up to Rotherham

The locks are very large and have powered operation of gates and paddles. All chambers have vertical bars set into the walls so that securing ropes can slide up and down with a boat. When locking upstream, it is advisable to keep boats away from the top gates as the turbulence can be excessive for small craft. Similarly, boats below a lock should not be near the bottom gates when it is emptying.

Don Navigation, Rotherham and above

See the maximum dimensions table opposite. Manual operation. Top paddles are often locked; operate with a BW (Watermate) key.

Sheffield & Tinsley Canal

The eleven wide locks of the Tinsley flight at Sheffield have two BW keepers who will help boat crews and take care of pumping water back up to the summit pound. Advance contact is appreciated (telephone number on page 94). Eastwood Lock is the nearest with a telephone.

Bridges

Stainforth & Keadby Canal

There are six boater-operated swing-bridges and one lift-bridge, plus another at Thorne Lock that forms part of the lock operation. All require a BW (Watermate) key; some are powered, others are manual effort. Instruction panels are by each bridge. At Keadby the road swing-bridge is operated by the BW lock-keepers, and the railway retracting bridge is controlled by rail staff.

New Junction Canal

There are four lift-bridges and three swing-bridges, including one across the chamber of Sykehouse Lock. All are normally boater-operated, although on busy summer weekends BW staff may operate Sykehouse Lock and some moveable bridges.

Don Navigation
One powered lift-bridge at Barnby Dun.

River Don
The River Don is used on some parts of the navigation above Doncaster. It's an easy boating waterway, but extra care is always needed on rivers — changes in level after heavy rain, tree branches etc. being washed along, mud deposited on the inside of bends, the flow affecting journey timings, and often a lack of towpath and moorings. Extra care should be taken in early spring and winter as rain and snow can swell water volumes in any river.

Supplies

Shopping
There are small general stores at Stainforth and Barnby Dun. Thorne is a market town with all facilities. There is a Tesco supermarket near the Doncaster BW moorings. Mexborough has all shops. Rotherham has two canal-side supermarkets — Asda at Aldwarke Lock, and Tesco by good moorings at Rotherham Lock — plus all the usual town stores and banks. Sheffield's Meadowhall retail park has over 270 shops, an 11-screen cinema and restaurants, but canal access is awaiting a bridge over the railway. Meanwhile the canal-side Supertram goes to Meadowhall from its stops near the Victoria Quay and Don Valley Stadium moorings.

Petrol and Diesel
Generally available; sites marked on maps.

Launderette
None.

Moorings
Official BW moorings are marked on the maps. On the three canals boats can moor by the towpath, but anglers will be present during the fishing season. It is recommended that official moorings be used on the river sections of the Don Navigation.

Pump-outs
BW machines at Long Sandall Lock and Sheffield Basin. Card-operated (see note about debit cards below).

Debit Cards
In this area BW is introducing a card system, similar to payphone cards, to operate pump-outs, showers, electricity hook-ups, etc. Cards are available from locks and BW offices. Latest details from BW Doncaster (page 94)

Slipways
Sheffield Canal Company
Strawberry Island Boat Club
Stanilands Marina
Blue Water Marina

British Waterways
Telephone numbers are on page 94.

Head of Navigation Plaque
A brass plaque is on sale at the Basin Master's office, Sheffield. Application forms are also available from the Tinsley lock-keepers and the BW office at Doncaster.

1991 IWA Campaign Festival at Sheffield

21

Control panel at Thorne Lock

The large mechanical lock at Eastwood dwarfs a typical narrowboat.

Exceptionally heavy rainfall can cause flooding on river sections, as seen here at Sprotbrough.

Moving Bridges

Low Lane Swing-Bridge

Wykewell Lift-Bridge

1. Lapwing; 2. Goldfinch; 3. Heron; 4. Kingfisher; 5. Great Crested Grebe (pictures not to scale)

Wildlife

The SSYN is remarkable for the major differences in habitat along its length, from city centre to remote lowlands.

The *Sheffield & Tinsley Canal* is the major body of 'standing water' in the city and attracts the wildlife suited to that environment rather than the flowing waters of the River Don. Thankfully the gross pollution of water, air and land is in the past.

The *New Junction Canal* has wide verges on both sides that are full of wildlife and summer flowers.

The richest environment is bordered by the *New Junction Canal*, the *Stainforth & Keadby Canal* and the River Ouse. There is a remarkable variety of wildlife thrives on the old flood-lands of the tidal rivers Don and Went; a mosaic of small damp pastures, hay meadows, a network of drainage ditches and old hedgerows. Some of this area (Thorne Moors) is controlled by English Nature.

Birds

Birdline North East (Tel: 0891 700246) gives recorded information on recent sightings in the area.

Sprotbrough Flash is a large lake by the navigation upstream of Sprotbrough lock. It is a nature reserve administered by Yorkshire Wildlife Trust and there are hides to watch the birds.

The following birds have been seen along the Navigation.

Black Redstart

Elusive black birds with lengthy red tails, these are often found near old buildings, hunting for insects on walls and in corners. In late spring the male starts to sing very early in the morning. A small breeding population in the lower Don valley stretches into Sheffield city centre.

Black Tern

The black tern passes through on migration in the summer and autumn, often stopping near shallow fresh water to rest and feed. They sometimes swoop for insects like a large swallow. They can be seen at Southfield Reservoir at the end of the New Junction Canal, especially in August.

Coot

These are large black birds usually seen swimming on the navigation, but also grazing on grasslands. A distinctive white patch covers the front of the head and top of the bill: the reason for the saying 'as bald as a coot'. The downy chicks have a red face and bill and, if seen apart from an adult, may be taken for moorhen young. Noisy splashy fights may occur when bordering territories meet. When hastily retreating, coots perform a mixture of running and flying across the surface of the water.

Curlew

The largest British wader, its body is about 18 inches long, its bill another 5 inches. The long legs and curved bill are unmistakable. They breed on Thorne Moor and go to the shore in the winter.

Goldfinch

The collective term is a 'charm' of goldfinches, and for good reason. The liquid notes of their song is charming and they are a splash of colour with their red, black and white heads, and gold-barred tails. They feed on thistles and when disturbed fly off with musical calls and circle back down. Often seen and heard canal-side in Sheffield and Rotherham.

Great Crested Grebe

This bird dives for food, sometimes disappearing for 30 seconds. It has distinctive ear-tufts and likes slow-flowing water and banks with plenty of reeds. The young are striped and cheep continuously.

Heron

Visible at all times of the year, these are the largest wild birds that can commonly be seen (discounting swans). They are most active at dusk and dawn, stalking slowly after fish, frogs, voles, insects, and eels. During the day they often stand motionless near the water's edge. They usually flap away at the last minute when disturbed. In flight the heron's size, long legs and bent neck make it unmistakable. They may also be seen in fields, and nesting in tall trees from February onwards.

Hobby

The hobby is one of the smallest falcons, and a summer visitor. They fly very fast and can catch swallows and swifts and groups of such birds often defend themselves by mobbing a hobby. Seen over Thorne Moor in July.

Kestrel

The commonest British falcon. Often seen hovering over the land alongside the Sheffield & Tinsley Canal, dropping like a stone onto its prey, mostly mice and voles.

25

Kingfisher

Usually seen as a brilliant flash of intense blue, flying at up to 25mph low to the water surface, wings rapidly whirring. When sitting motionless watching for fish from a branch over the water, they are surprisingly difficult to see. Canals and slower-moving rivers where there are fish are preferred, and sandy banks are needed for nest burrows. They are often seen in Rotherham at Jordan Lock Weir and by the river Don in Sheffield.

Lapwing

A small wader with a distinctive crest. They nest on Thorne Moor and large flocks can be seen flying over the adjacent canals. Also known as the peewit because that is what its call sounds like.

Little Grebe

Found on quieter stretches in winter, these are small dumpy birds that dive at the first sign of danger. They feed by diving to catch small fish. Also known as the dabchick.

Marsh Harrier

This is the largest British harrier, about 20 inches long. They are seen in flight over Thorne Moor, low over the reeds, gliding and then gaining speed with a few deliberate wingbeats.

Moorhen

Moorhens are black birds with a red bill and front of head. They are usually seen swimming, but are adaptable and can climb trees, walk on flat ground, and clamber through undergrowth. One of the few birds to swim well without webbed feet. From April to July the nests are conspicuous floating mats of dried vegetation, close to the water's edge. They prefer the quieter water of canals to flowing rivers.

Nightingale

Nightingales are difficult to see because they keep to thick cover, but the famous song is unmistakable: a mixture of long drawn-out notes that poets often thought 'sad', delivered in sudden loud bursts. The breeding population near the canal on Thorne Moor is the most northerly in the world.

Nightjar

These are summer visitors that catch insects on the wing. The male's jarring song (hence the name) goes on for several minutes, rising and falling, and may be heard by the canal from Thorne Moor.

Shoveler

A duck with a green head like a mallard, but a very broad bill. They breed near the canal at Thorne.

Snipe

A wader with a long bill, the snipe breeds on the land between the New Junction Canal and the Stainforth & Keadby Canal. They gather in large flocks in the winter.

Spoonbill

Unmistakable summer visitors to Thorne Moor. Nearly 3 feet long, they stand and sweep their wide bills through still water, gripping anything edible. They have a graceful flapping flight and also glide and soar.

Animals

The Sheffield & Tinsley Canal has *water voles*, *smooth newts* and *common frogs*, as well as *foxes*, *rabbits*, *stoats*, *weasels* and *shrews* on the surrounding land. A dinnerplate-sized *terrapin* is sometimes seen near Staniforth Road Bridge.

Deer are often seen near the New Junction Canal, and the Stainforth & Keadby Canal. They sometimes fall into the water and special escape ramps are being provided as they have difficulty climbing out over the steep banks. There is one near Maud's Bridge (Map 11).

Bats fly over the water in many areas, feeding on the insects that congregate there at dusk.

Insects

The caterpillar of the *elephant hawk moth* is often on rosebay willowherb, whereas the caterpillar of the *cinnabar moth* prefers ragwort and groundsel.

A good selection of butterflies may be seen: *meadow brown*, *wall brown*, *orange tip*, *small tortoiseshell*, *peacocks*. *Common blues* are often found near birdsfoot trefoil growing in the short grass by the towpath.

Meadow grasshoppers, brown *hawker dragonflies*, and blue-tailed *damselflies* are common.

Plants

Sheffield Canal

Local botanists have recorded over 80 different plants, for many such as the narrow-leaved *water plantain* this is the only location in Sheffield. *Reedmace* and *yellow flag iris* fringe much of the area. Waste land colonisers also thrive: *rosebay willowherb, ragwort, coltsfoot;* and *soapwort,* the leaves and stem of which used to be mashed and boiled to produce a liquid soap used to wash woollen cloth. *Wallflowers, lupins* and *michaelmas daisies* are garden escapees.

New Junction Canal

Water figwort, and clumps of tangerine-scented *sweet flag.* Near the Went Aqueduct are lush beds of *reed sweet-grass,* beloved of grazing cattle. On the water's edge and ditch sides are *soft rush, false fox sedge, marsh pennywort, reed grass, great willowherb, meadowsweet, angelica,* and *woody nightshade.*

Between the New Junction Canal and the Stainforth & Keadby Canal

Some boundary hedgerows are Elizabethan; a few are Norman, made up of numerous different types of shrubs and plants. Common trees are *oak, field maple, ash,* and ancient *white willows.* Typical marshy site plants are *water plantain, reedmace, starworts,* and poisonous *water dropworts.*

Fish

Bream

A shy fish that forms large shoals and frequents deep water, moves into shallows at night to feed. A deep body with a brown back, golden-brown sides, and brown fins. Average 9–16 inches.

Carp

Prefers weedy areas, and forms small shoals. Usually swims near the bottom, but on warm summer days will often bask lazily near the surface. Greenish-brown back, yellowish-brown sides, and small barbels at each side of mouth. Females grow to 9–19 inches.

Chub

The young form shoals, but older fish are solitary. Dark grey-green back, greenish sides, and red lower fins. Feeds on other fish as well as plants and insects. About 16 inches.

Gudgeon

Bottom-living small fish, prefers slow-flowing water. Feeds on insect larvae and crustaceans. Slender body, greeny-brown back, yellowish sides with round dusky patches, spotted fins. Usually 4–6 inches.

Perch

The most abundant European fish. The young form shoals under bridges or leaning trees; older fish are more solitary. Slow-moving. Brownish-green back with dark bars across it, yellow-green sides, and red lower fins; 8–11 inches.

Roach

A member of the carp family. Feeds on small water insects and aquatic plants, mainly on the bottom. A dark rounded back, intensely silver sides, reddish eyes, and red fins. Average 6–10 inches.

Mute swan

A view of Sheffield from Meersbrook Park

Sheffield

Sheffield is Britain's fifth largest city. It is famous the world over for cutlery, tools, blades and special steels. A modern working city in a country setting, fringed by the Peak District National Park, Sheffield itself spreads up and down five main rivers and seven great hills.

The major renovation of the canal basin is part of the development plans that are breathing new life into the city. The Supertram system and the major sports venues are the most evident signs of this regeneration, although the effects of track-laying for Supertram along the major roads has been quite traumatic.

There are many art galleries, museums, historic buildings and theatres. The Crucible Theatre is famous for the World Snooker Championships. An audio-guided Walkman Tour of the city centre takes about an hour, complete with commentary and special sound effects. The equipment can be hired from the Tourist Information Centre at the railway station.

From the bus station many routes go out to the surrounding countryside and villages that make Sheffield's 'golden frame'.

Swimming at Ponds Forge

Near the canal basin, Ponds Forge has a leisure pool with a wave machine, 'lazy river' and two 80-metre suspended flumes. The international pool is Olympic size; the separate diving area is the deepest competition pool in the world; and there is a swimwear shop. The telephone number is on page 94.

CITY CENTRE

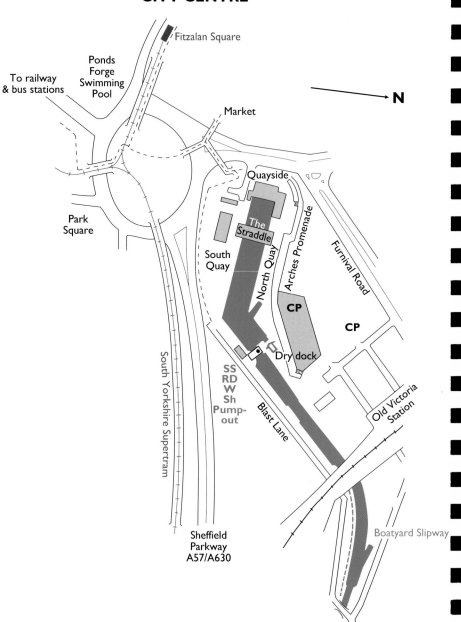

Fitzalan Square

Ponds Forge Swimming Pool

To railway & bus stations

Market

N

Quayside

Park Square

The Straddle

South Quay

North Quay

Arches Promenade

Furnival Road

CP

CP

Dry dock

South Yorkshire Supertram

SS RD W Sh Pump- out

Blast Lane

Old Victoria Station

Sheffield Parkway A57/A630

Boatyard Slipway

Victoria Quays (Sheffield Basin)

Past

The oldest building in the basin is Quayside, once the four-storey Terminal Warehouse. This was constructed in 1819 when the canal was completed. Attached to it is the Grain Warehouse, late 19th century, with a bucket elevator used until 1972. These buildings are masked by The Straddle, another warehouse added in 1895. Up to five barges could stop underneath to allow their cargoes to be hoisted into the building.

On North Quay were the offices of coal merchants and the canal company where the boatmen took bills of lading for signature and paid their canal dues. Transhipped goods were also stored under the railway arches. South Quay had large sheds where cargoes of Scandinavian timber were kept.

In the late 1960s the head of commercial navigation was moved to Rotherham and the last cargo into Sheffield Basin was a load of maize in December 1970. For the next twenty years the basin was used for mooring private boats, but the buildings were empty and decaying. The renovation work began in 1993; during the following two years the basin has been converted into Victoria Quays.

Present

(as planned at the time of writing)

In the 1980s the Sheffield Development Corporation started to renovate the industry-ravaged valley of the River Don and the canal corridor. The vast Meadowhall shopping complex was an early project. In 1993 they turned their attention to the canal basin, using it as the centre of plans to rejuvenate the surrounding city area.

The Terminal and Grain warehouses, and the old offices and railway arches are now known as Quayside — including pub, restaurant, and speciality shopping. The Straddle Warehouse is now high-profile office accommodation, augmented by new buildings on South Quay. A walkway from the basin entrance gives traffic-free access to Supertram and the city centre.

Moorings for boats have been provided and a dry-dock discovered during the renovation work might be used to display a feature vessel.

Navigation

Boat traffic and mooring is controlled by the British Waterways Basin Master, from the BW building near the swing-bridge. If wishing to stay in the basin, prior notice of arrival is recommended; the telephone number is on page 94.

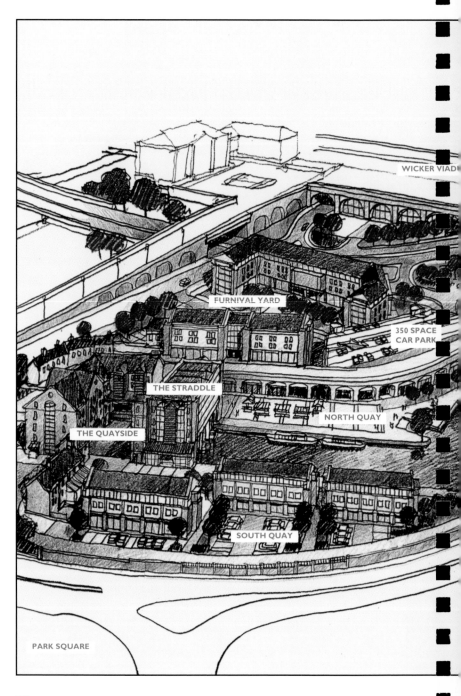

WICKER VIAD[UCT]

FURNIVAL YARD

350 SPACE CAR PARK

THE STRADDLE

NORTH QUAY

THE QUAYSIDE

SOUTH QUAY

PARK SQUARE

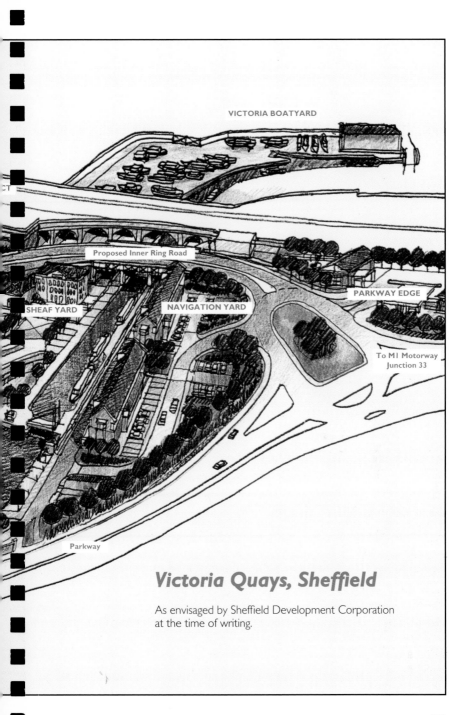

VICTORIA BOATYARD

Proposed Inner Ring Road

PARKWAY EDGE

SHEAF YARD

NAVIGATION YARD

To MI Motorway
Junction 33

Parkway

Victoria Quays, Sheffield

As envisaged by Sheffield Development Corporation
at the time of writing.

Map I: *Sheffield & Tinsley Canal*
Sheffield – M I
3.5 miles

General Area
This is a typical city canal — lined with a mixture of old buildings from an industrial past and the modern structures of present regeneration and change. Eighty plant types have been recorded on the grassy banks which, in autumn, are covered in purple asters. At the head of navigation the old canal basin has been completely renovated and renamed Victoria Quays. The new Supertram system has improved access to the towpath between the city and Tinsley Locks. Downstream of Worksop Road Aqueduct there are views over the city, and two new stadiums stand where steelworks used to be. The eleven Tinsley locks link the canal's summit pound to the River Don.

Cadman Street and Bacon Lane Bridges
These are the only two original bridges remaining. Bacon Lane is the tightest on the canal and therefore determines the size of boats reaching the basin. When empty, the old keels were sometimes lowered by opening sea-cocks and taking on twenty tons of water, then levered through the bridge by using a crowbar; when through, the water was hand-pumped out again.

Attercliffe (Darnall) Cutting
150 yards long, 36 feet deep, dug by men unemployed in the recession at the end of the Napoleonic Wars. The Overseers of the Poor supplied plenty of labour and this made the excavation rapid and cheap.

Don Valley Stadium
An international athletics stadium. It is also the home of Sheffield Eagles RLFC.

Sheffield Arena
The Arena stages concerts, and is home to the Sheffield Steelers (ice hockey). The 'scrap basket' on a nearby mound is a reminder of the steelworks previously on this site.

Tinsley Locks
In 1994 the keepers won a British Waterways prize for the improvements made. Access to the nearby Supertram stop (Carbrook) is through the tunnel by Lock 3.

Tinsley Locks 4 and 5
These were hit by German bombs on 15th December 1940; Lock 5 was damaged and the keeper's ornate castellated house by Lock 4 was destroyed. The canal burst and drained into the river and boats were stranded for many weeks.

Meadowhall Shopping Centre
This shopping complex contains over 270 shops, an 11-screen cinema, and restaurants. A bridge over the railway is planned for direct access from the canal; otherwise catch a Supertram at Lock 3.

Navigation
Sheffield Basin
See page 31.

Bacon Lane Bridge
The most restrictive on the Navigation (see page 20).

Tinsley Flight
Now eleven locks, originally twelve. Rise/fall 96 feet in 1.5 miles; manual operation; standard windlass; BW (Watermate) key for paddles. There are two keepers on duty; with advance notice they will help craft through the flight; the telephone number is on page 94. They also pump water back up to feed the summit pound. Lock 7 is two merged locks and has the deepest chamber; the paddle-gear winds anti-clockwise and should be opened slowly; the gates are heavy.

Walking
The towpath is complete, but for security reasons it may not reach directly into the restored basin (Victoria Quays). If so, a road route between the main basin entrance and the towpath will be signposted along Blast Lane. The new Supertrams are a good means of return transport with three stations near to the towpath (see page 93). At the Carbrook stop, towpath access is over the footbridge at the platform end, then through a short tunnel.

Five Weirs Walk
See page 18.

SHEFFIELD CITY CENTRE

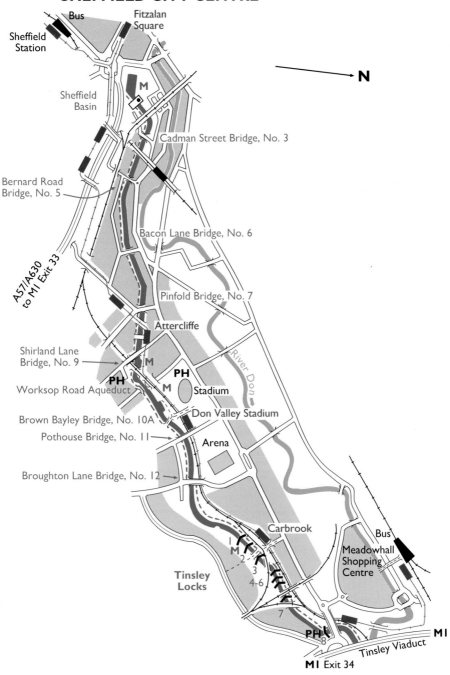

Bus

Fitzalan Square

Sheffield Station

Sheffield Basin

M

Cadman Street Bridge, No. 3

Bernard Road Bridge, No. 5

Bacon Lane Bridge, No. 6

A57/A630 to M1 Exit 33

Pinfold Bridge, No. 7

Attercliffe

Shirland Lane Bridge, No. 9

M

PH

PH

Worksop Road Aqueduct

M

Stadium

Brown Bayley Bridge, No. 10A

Don Valley Stadium

Pothouse Bridge, No. 11

Arena

Broughton Lane Bridge, No. 12

River Don

Carbrook

Bus

Meadowhall Shopping Centre

1

M

2

3

4-6

Tinsley Locks

7

PH

8

M1

M1 Exit 34

Tinsley Viaduct

N

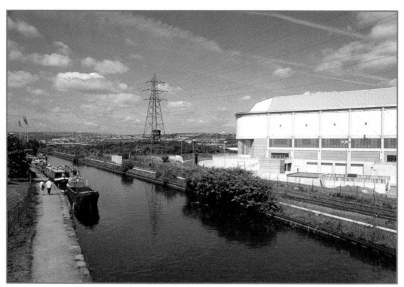

Sheffield Arena

Trent sloop Amy Howson *at the 1991 IWA Campaign Festival, Sheffield*

Tinsley Locks

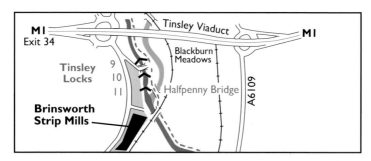

Moorings and a preserved coal-loading chute, Rotherham

Unloading steel, Rawmarsh Road Depot, Rotherham

Map 2: *Don Navigation*
MI – Parkgate (Rotherham)
3.5 miles

General Area
The area is changing now heavy industry has gone. Between Jordan and Ickles locks, a joint Rotherham Council and British Waterways scheme has already included tree planting, angling facilities, large-scale renovation and a new towpath. Further improvements are planned, including a towpath through Rotherham town centre. Blackburn Meadows Nature Reserve is nearing completion next to Holmes Lock. Rotherham has a wide mixture of canal-side buildings — old warehouses and cranes, new police station and magistrates court, back yards of commercial premises, and a supermarket.

Halfpenny Bridge
A man in a little hut collected a toll of one halfpenny from men using the bridge to go to work.

Holmes Goit
This used to be a water supply to nearby iron and steel mills.

Blackburn Meadows Nature Reserve
Free access, with lakes, bird-hides, recreated wetlands habitat, and a windmill that pumps water into the lakes. The impressive heron-topped gates are the work of local Andy Ball and are a reminder of the steelworks that used to occupy the site.

Steel Street Bridge
There are tram-tracks in its cobbled roadway.

Walker Branch
Only the stone portal remains. It was a link between an old cut and the Holmes Works of Walker & Co., the first large ironworks in Rotherham.

River Rother
Until the early 1970s grain barges went to the flour mill just upstream of the junction with the Don.

Warehouses
Near the rail station are two old warehouses with chutes nearby for loading boats moored below; one has a crane alongside. The warehouses are now used by a pine furniture retailer and a grain merchant.

Boat Launch Tragedy
In July 1841 a Rotherham festival celebrated the launching of a boat. Many children went to watch and some were among the 150 people on the boat as it went down the slipway. The new vessel immediately capsized, trapping the passengers underneath and fifty of them drowned.

Rawmarsh Road Depot
(Head of commercial navigation)
In 1980 this was planned to be a 'bustling trans-shipment dock handling 0.5 million tons of freight a year'. This is the sorry result of the delayed modernisation scheme, the remains of the 'Rotherport' dreams. (See 'History' chapter, page 11.)

Navigation
Halfpenny Bridge is the head of navigation on the River Don. Locks: manual operation; standard windlass; BW (Watermate) key to open top paddles. *Holmes Lock* is sometimes difficult as balance beams have been modified near the bridge. *Ickles Lock* has extensive good moorings. *Rotherham Lock* is the first/last manually operated lock, as are all the rest up to Sheffield.

Shopping
Tesco supermarket is beside Rotherham Lock and moorings, with access via the bridge over the lock; it contains a newsagent and pharmacy, and closes daily 20.00; open Sunday 10.00–16.00.

Walking
Take the footbridge over the River Don at the foot of Tinsley Locks, and walk across Holmes Goit alongside Jordan Lock. Between Tinsley Locks and Ickles Lock there is a new wide towpath, to be extended to Greasbrough Road Bridge by 1995. Beyond the bridge a second phase is planned, dependent on European funding.

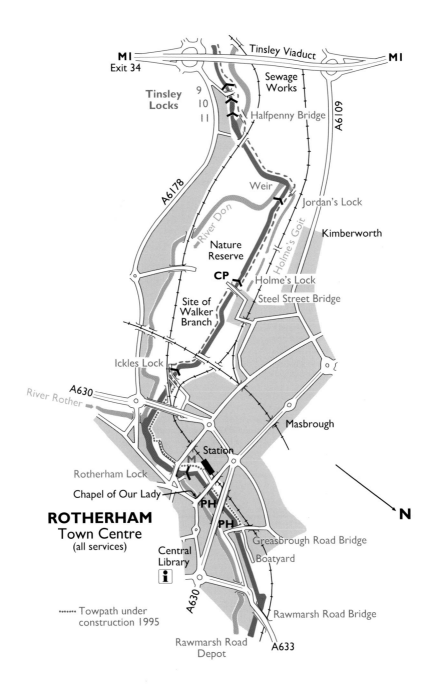

MI
Exit 34

Tinsley Viaduct

MI

Sewage Works

Tinsley Locks

9
10
11

Halfpenny Bridge

A6109

A6178

Weir

Jordan's Lock

River Don

Holme's Goit

Kimberworth

Nature Reserve

CP

Holme's Lock

Steel Street Bridge

Site of Walker Branch

Ickles Lock

A630

River Rother

Masbrough

Station

M

Rotherham Lock

Chapel of Our Lady

PH

N

PH

ROTHERHAM
Town Centre
(all services)

Greasbrough Road Bridge

Central Library
ℹ️

Boatyard

A630

········ Towpath under construction 1995

Rawmarsh Road Bridge

Rawmarsh Road Depot

A633

New magistrates' court by Rotherham Lock

Ickles Lock

Rotherham

All shops and banks, etc. can be found in Rotherham. Market days are on Mondays, Fridays and Saturdays.

Rotherham, at the junction of the rivers Don and Rother, grew because coal and iron ore were found locally. Now it's Rotherham that makes most of the specialised steel in the area, not Sheffield — as any proud local will tell you. But such industry is not near the town centre and the shops are spread along pedestrianised areas that are bedecked with flowers in the summer. In 1993 Rotherham was the outright national winner of the 'Britain in Bloom' cities category.

At the centre of the town is the *Parish Church of All Saints*, mainly dating from the 15th century and one of the finest examples of perpendicular architecture in Yorkshire. A smaller religious building is the *Chapel of Our Lady* on the bridge over the Don, adjacent to the SSYN. It was used by travellers praying for God's blessing on their journey and is one of only three remaining bridge chapels in the country, still used for services each Tuesday. The river's channel has been moved and the old chapel is now on dry land.

The town-centre *Clifton Park* has one of the country's finest amusement parks for children, a paddling pool and miniature train rides, as well as bowls, putting, tennis and crazy golf. *Clifton Park Museum* has an enviable collection of the world-famous Rockingham pottery which was made locally.

The Central Library building contains the *York and Lancaster Regimental Museum* and the *Tourist Information Centre*.

The Chapel of Our Lady on Chantry Bridge, Rotherham

Map 3: *Don Navigation*
Parkgate (Rotherham) – Kilnhurst
4 miles

General Area
Heavy industry is on both banks, but little can be seen of it behind high bushes. A power station is fronted by abundant wild flowers; fine willow trees hide the source of the crashes and bleeps that go on beyond them. Steelworks with yellow cranes on gantries, and a pall of dust and steam, can sometimes be seen. Massive dark grey sheds are certainly visible, stretching on and on. On the opposite bank new trees have been planted, and nearby older trees and bushes overhang both banks.

Greasbrough Canal
Also known as the Parkgate Canal, and the Earl Fitzwilliam Canal, it was built by engineer William Jessop in 1780 to carry coal from local pits. It was only 1.5 miles long and was last used c. 1918. Half a mile was renovated as a fishery in 1986 and both banks of that section can be walked.

Eastwood Lock
The official name is Sir Frank Price Lock, the British Waterways Chairman at the time of the 1980s modernisation. Moorings alongside are where two old locks used to be.

Aldwarke Bridge
A single-span sandstone bridge rebuilt in 1834. A listed structure.

Steelworks
Basic new steel from iron ore is no longer made in Rotherham or Sheffield; that is now done at Scunthorpe. Instead, high-quality and specialised engineering steel is made by melting down scrap metal. The annual steel tonnage produced along the Don Valley now is greater than it was during the peak years of World War II, with an eighth of the workforce and minimal pollution.

Kilnhurst Lock
The old derelict lock alongside the new lock predates the 1980s modernisation.

Navigation

Eastwood Lock
This is the first/last powered lock, with a keeper on duty at busy times; otherwise it is crew-operated with a BW (Watermate) key. The water point is by the lock cabin. If you are going to use the eleven Tinsley locks, phone the flight-keepers from here (see page 94), and they will be ready to help you operate the manual locks. This is the last lock with a telephone, found at the front of the cabin. Calls can also be made from Rotherham town centre.

Aldwarke Bridge
Headroom may be limited for large craft if river levels are high.

Aldwarke Lock
A powered lock, crew-operated with a BW (Watermate) key. The paddles open in timed bursts when the button is pressed once. Below the lock the landing stage is just past the lock entrance where the river comes in from the weir.

Shopping
There is an Asda supermarket beside Aldwarke Lock; access is via the gate with a BW (Watermate) key near the bottom of the lock. You will also find cashpoints (Lloyd's, Barclay's), shoe repairs, hair salon, café, pharmacy, and recycling point (cans, bottles, plastic, newspapers, etc). It closes daily at 20.00, and opens on Sunday 10.00–16.00. You can also get petrol and there is a McDonald's.

Kilnhurst Lock
A small rise/fall depending on river levels above. A powered lock, crew-operated with a BW (Watermate) key. The water supply for the canal from here to Mexborough passes through this lock; when not being used by boats the paddles may automatically rise at both ends to maintain the supply. When the control panel is first activated by a crew, the lock will automatically reset itself for boat use. Until this is done, the usual procedures will not commence. This also applies to Doncaster Town Lock further downstream

Rail Bridge
Blind bend, both directions.

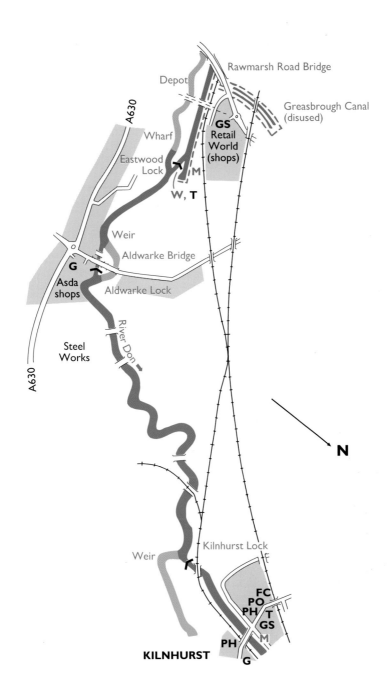

Rawmarsh Road Bridge

Depot

Greasbrough Canal
(disused)

A630

Wharf

GS
Retail
World
(shops)

Eastwood
Lock

M

W, T

Weir

Aldwarke Bridge

G

Asda
shops

Aldwarke Lock

River Don

Steel
Works

A630

N

Weir

Kilnhurst Lock

FC
PO
PH

T

GS

M

PH

KILNHURST

G

The Greasbrough Canal

Eastwood Lock

On the river above Kilnhurst Lock

Map 4: *Don Navigation*
Kilnhurst – Mexborough Low Lock
3.5 miles

General Area
Near Kilnhurst there are various works and houses on opposite banks. Nearer to Swinton, industrial sites line the west bank, a complete contrast to the eastern side where open countryside spreads across to the hills on the far valley side. Between the two Mexborough locks there is a mixture of houses, roads, light industry and gardens. As the downstream valley opens out, Mexborough can be seen on a small hill with the navigation winding around its base.

Dearne & Dove Canal
Built in the 1790s, it is mostly abandoned, but the Barnsley Canal Group are working for its restoration. The flight of locks near Swinton Lock is used as dry-docks by Waddington's boatyard. Restoration schemes may use the River Dearne to bypass this area.

Swinton Lock
Its official name is Waddington Lock in honour of the Swinton boat company, owner of the moored commercial craft.

Swinton Station
This was the railway limit for eight years from 1840. Rail passengers boarded boats called 'aquabuses' for the rest of their journey to Doncaster, the fares of one shilling for the best cabin and 9d for the fore-cabin were half the road coach rates. The aquabuses also called at Conisbrough and Sprotbrough.

Old Barnsley British Co-op Bakery
Canal-side with a wharf and hoist where supplies were unloaded from boats.

Ferry Boat Lane, Mexborough
The site of the river ferry is by the ramp of the footbridge above Mexborough Top Lock. There is a winch and a stone marked with river flood levels and 'ask for boat at cabin' (see photographs on page 15). The ferry service ran for over 300 years, ending in 1964 when the adjacent bridge was built.

Locks
When the old keels passed through a lock, the boatmen operated one side of the chamber, the lock-keeper the other side. The boatmen threw a penny onto the lockside for the keeper, although he was paid by the navigation company. When going upstream, masts and sails were left with the Mexborough lock-keeper, and collected on the way back. Numerous upstream fixed bridges meant sailing was inefficient because the masts had to be lowered too often, so a horse and handler — a horse-marine — was hired here.

Navigation

Swinton Lock

Powered; crew-operated with a BW (Watermate) key. Keep your boat back from the bottom gates when the lock is emptying. Large commercial craft are often moored in the vicinity.

Rail Bridge

Sharp blind bend, both directions.

Yorkshire Rose Marina

Canal-side moorings and a hire-boat, and a welcome from owner Trevor Crompton (see page 94).

Mexborough

Market days are Monday, Friday and Saturday. All shops; best access from Yorkshire Rose Marina.

Mexborough Top Lock

Powered; a keeper on duty at busy times. Otherwise crew-operated with a BW (Watermate) key.

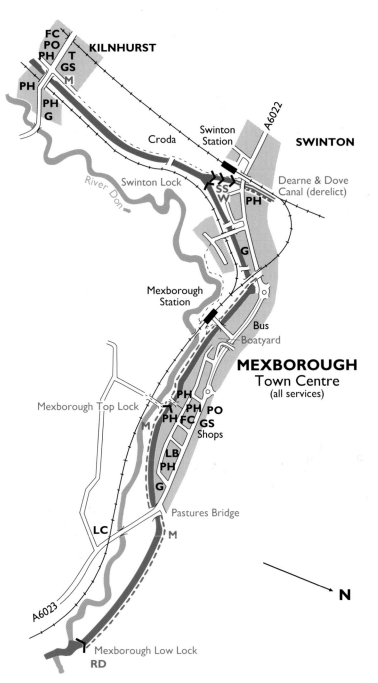

KILNHURST

FC
PO
PH
T
GS
M
PH
PH
G

Croda

Swinton
Station

SWINTON

A6022

Dearne & Dove
Canal (derelict)

River Don

Swinton Lock

SS
W
PH

G

Mexborough
Station

Bus

Boatyard

MEXBOROUGH
Town Centre
(all services)

Mexborough Top Lock

PH
PH
PH FC
PO
GS
Shops

M

LB
PH

G

Pastures Bridge

LC

M

A6023

Mexborough Low Lock
RD

N

The derelict Dearne & Dove Canal at Swinton

E.V. Waddington's depot and moorings at Swinton Junction

Mexborough Top Lock

Mexborough

Map 5: *Don Navigation*
Mexborough Low Lock – A1
4 miles

General Area
Between Mexborough Low Lock and Conisbrough the scenery is a bit scruffy, the result of past industrial use of the valley, but this will change when the Earth Centre complex is completed. The open valley where Conisbrough and its castle look down at the river is replaced by a narrower downstream gorge. Between Conisbrough and Sprotbrough there are greenery-covered banks with shrubs and wild flowers. The river winds gently in a narrow valley between hills, both banks wooded, the trees hanging over the water's edge. No other signs of life are evident — no houses or roads, the railway hidden from view. Limestone outcrops can sometimes be seen through the trees. The wooded scenery continues between the lock and the A1 bridge.

The Earth Centre
Two former colliery sites are being transformed into an environmental visitor park on a 200-acre site. The first phase is due to open in July 1995 with a visitor centre, wetlands, aquatic centre, and wildlife projects. There will eventually be the 'Ride of Life', 'The Solar Age', and 'Inside the Whale'. Access from the river is planned.

Conisbrough Castle
English Heritage. A unique example of a 12th-century fortress, its magnificent 90ft-high keep virtually intact and re-roofed. There is a visual presentation, visitor centre, and tea rooms. Open all year. The telephone number is on page 94.

Conisbrough Lock
Removed in 1972 because it only had a 15-inch rise/fall. The levels were maintained by increasing Sprotbrough Weir by the same amount. A brick wall with ironwork on top is all that remains.

Sprotbrough Flash
A nature reserve administered by the Yorkshire Wildlife Trust. Birds can be watched from hides, containing copious information, accessible from the towpath.

Sprotbro' Painter
Artist Sheila Bury's narrowboat — her floating gallery — it is normally moored near Sprotbrough road bridge.

Water Bus
Trips to Doncaster and Conisbrough from Sprotbrough. Operated by Alan Oliver Cruises (see page 94 and advert on page 60).

Sprotbrough
The area by the bridge is popular with local people at weekends. Boat Lane and the Boat Inn both owe their name to the ferry that operated here before the bridge was built. Between the lock and the A1 the remains of an old water-powered mill are fenced off by the towpath.

Navigation
Mexborough Low Lock

Powered; a keeper on duty at busy times; otherwise crew-operated with a BW (Watermate) key. Rubbish disposal is available; ask the keeper. The water point is inconveniently situated, and has a non-standard fitting. The rivers Don and Dearne come in below the lock; allow for effect in times of high flows.

Sprotbrough Lock

Powered; a keeper on duty at busy times; otherwise crew-operated with a BW (Watermate) key. Moorings are available upstream of the road bridge; if staying overnight, allow for possible level changes in the river if rainfall has been exceptionally heavy.

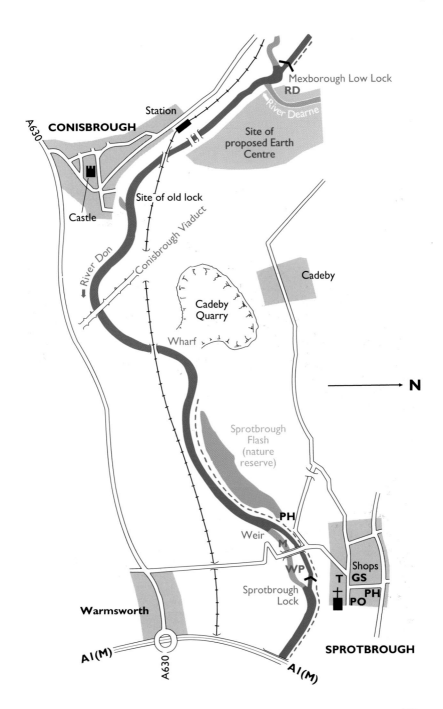

Mexborough Low Lock

RD

River Dearne

Station

CONISBROUGH

A630

Site of proposed Earth Centre

Castle

Site of old lock

River Don

Conisbrough Viaduct

Cadeby

Cadeby Quarry

Wharf

N

Sprotbrough Flash (nature reserve)

PH

Weir

M

WP

Sprotbrough Lock

Shops
GS

T
✝
PO

PH

Warmsworth

A1(M)

A630

A1(M)

SPROTBROUGH

British Waterways' craft, Kilnhurst Lock

A Commercial Waterway

The majority of the SSYN is still used by commercial craft: that is the Don Navigation downstream of Rotherham, the whole of the New Junction Canal, and perhaps the western end of the Stainforth & Keadby Canal.

The delays to the modernisation of the SSYN in the 1980s meant that a great opportunity to expand commercial use of the system was lost. However, two companies are still based on the SSYN — Alan Oliver at Sprotbrough, and Waddington's at Swinton. In addition, vessels from the Aire & Calder Navigation may also be present, for example the push-pull compartment-boat trains of Cawoods-Hargreaves. Each company paints the upperworks of its vessels a different colour — red = Alan Oliver; blue = Waddington's;

black and white = Cawoods-Hargreaves; green = British Waterways.

Cargoes and contracts vary. At the time of writing they include every six weeks 1,000 tons of fluorspar from Goole on the Aire & Calder, along the New Junction Canal and up to Rotherham. In 1995 60,000 tons of steel will be carried between Goole and Rotherham. Flux for steelmaking is also carried, and limestone is occasionally collected from Cadeby Quarry near Sprotbrough. Trial runs of coal have taken place from Hatfield Colliery, along the Stainforth & Keadby Canal and the New Junction Canal to Ferrybridge Power Station on the Aire & Calder. If this continues, it will be operated by Cawoods-Hargreaves.

Conisbrough Castle

Conisbrough Viaduct

Wyre Lady *and other Alan Oliver commercial craft moored above Sprotbrough Lock*

Map 6: *Don Navigation*
A1 – Strawberry Island
4 miles

General Area
The Navigation is the river here and its more natural course winds through the lowest levels of the Yorkshire hills. The sweeping bend is lined by a timber-covered ridge, with the houses of Balby peeping over the trees. It is a lovely stretch with the flood-meadows of Sprotbrough Ings behind a grass-covered floodbank. On the very edge of Doncaster the ancient farming hamlet of Newton perches on the riverbank. Doncaster still keeps its distance from a river that used to flood, with only railway and industrial sites — and the new prison — coming near.

Newton Hamlet
A ferry used to operate from here. Until 1947 Tom Vickers took passengers across the river in his smallish row-boat for 1d.

Railway Works
Many steam locomotives were built in Doncaster's extensive railway workshops, including the famous *Flying Scotsman* and *Mallard*. The same buildings are now a national railway spares and repairs centre.

Doncaster Prison
Opened in 1994 and run by a private company. Because its site is almost an island, it's known locally as 'Doncatraz'.

Power Station Bight
The prison is on the site once occupied by Doncaster Power Station. Until 1981 its coal supplies were brought by boat and the bight is where they were unloaded. The craft usually moored there now belong to Waddington's, a company based at Swinton Lock. The owner believes the return to water transport is inevitable — and his fleet is ready.

Doncaster Lock
The old sailing keels were sometimes 'freshbound' here for as long as a week, waiting for the fresh water in a flooded river to subside.

Old Canal Depot
By Friar's Gate Bridge, with a loading canopy and lettering on the end wall. Now occupied by electrical wholesalers.

Gas House Bight
A section of the old route, retained for boats serving a now-demolished gasworks. May soon be infilled.

Navigation
River
The river is used for 7 miles. The flow can be very fast after prolonged heavy rain. The safe haven of Sprotbrough Lock and moorings is approximately halfway through this stretch. If unsure, ask at the BW Doncaster Office before proceeding to the lock.

Hexthorpe
Rowing-eights sometimes present.

Doncaster Prison
Mooring is strictly prohibited alongside the prison walls.

Doncaster Lock
Powered; a keeper on duty at busy times; otherwise crew-operated with a BW (Watermate) key. The bottom gates and mooring bollards are dark under a road/rail bridge. The lock traffic lights are before the bridge. The water supply for the entire downstream navigation passes through this lock; when not being used by boats, the paddles may automatically rise at both ends to maintain the supply. When the control panel is first activated by a crew, the lock will automatically reset itself for boat use. Until this is done, the usual procedures will not commence. This also applies to Kilnhurst Lock further upstream.

British Waterways Office
Moorings are adjacent, and these are the best moorings for the town. A BW (Watermate) key allows you into the compound.

Strawberry Island Boat Club
The club is sorry but hire-boats are not allowed into the very crowded moorings. There is a slipway. The telephone number is on page 94.

Walking
At Newton it is worth walking through the ancient hamlet instead of using the riverside path with its steep drop and stiles. Between Church View road bridge and opposite Strawberry Island the towpath is currently not really walkable.

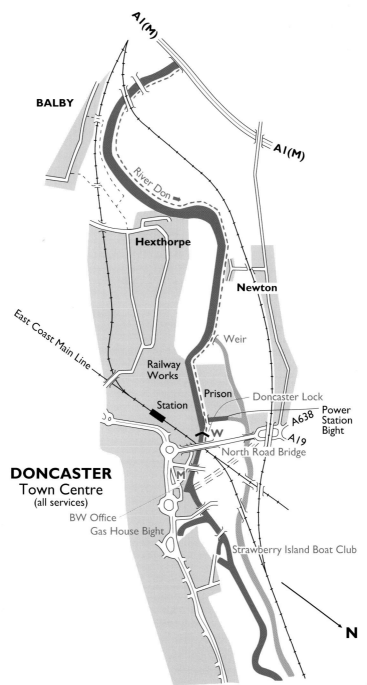

A1(M)

BALBY

A1(M)

River Don

Hexthorpe

Newton

East Coast Main Line

Weir

Railway Works

Prison

Doncaster Lock

Station

Power Station Bight

A638

A19

North Road Bridge

DONCASTER
Town Centre
(all services)

BW Office

Gas House Bight

Strawberry Island Boat Club

N

Doncaster

Doncaster is a busy town on the edge of South Yorkshire, originally a settlement at the lowest crossing point on the River Don. Throughout its history it has maintained a link with the Great North Road: the Romans built a fort on the route here and named it 'Danum', and in the Middle Ages Doncaster was an important trading centre and marketplace. In the 18th century the town was a major coaching centre on the London–Scotland road. Today the A1(M) passes nearby to the west.

In the 19th century Doncaster became a major railway centre and many steam locomotives were built — including the *Flying Scotsman* and the world-record-breaking *Mallard*. The buildings are now a national rail spares and repairs centre, and there is a 90-minute rail service to London.

There has been a racecourse at Doncaster since at least 1600 and it has been the home of the St Leger, the oldest of the English Classic horse races, since 1776.

The town centre has many fine buildings — the Mansion House in High Street, the shops in Hallgate, Georgian houses on South Parade and the neo-Gothic church of St George.

Covered and open-air markets with over 650 stalls are held every week: general items on Tuesdays, Thursdays, Fridays and Saturdays; antiques and bric-a-brac on Wednesdays. There are many inns and pubs around the marketplace. Unfortunately the adjacent Corn Exchange was badly damaged by fire in 1994 and is being restored.

The shopping areas are mainly pedestrianised with three modern centres: Frenchgate, The Colonnades, and Waterdale.

There are many country parks, gardens and nature reserves in the surrounding areas. The popular Museum of South Yorkshire Life at Cusworth Hall Country Park is just to the west of the town.

Strawberry Island Boat Club

Map 7: *Don Navigation*
Strawberry Island – Barnby Dun
4 miles

General Area
On the outskirts of Doncaster the proximity of the River Don keeps one bank clear of the string of industrial sites that line the other. The river and the navigation, and the flood-meadows beyond, form an open corridor through an urban area, although the river's floodbanks restrict the views for boat crews. Upstream to the south-west can be seen distant Yorkshire hills.

Long Sandall Lock
There used to be two smaller locks side by side, and a weir into the river. The second old lock is alongside the new large chamber and is now used for official BW moorings. In 1994 keeper Graham Barass won third prize in BW's best-kept waterway length (north-east) competition.

River Don
This area is the limit of the tide on the river.

Kirk Sandall
Pilkington's Glassworks dominates the scene with a high gantry across the canal and the high-banked river. The attractive church of St Oswald's on the canal bank is now redundant, the residential centre of the village having moved away from the waterway.

Navigation

Long Sandall Lock
Powered; keeper on duty at busy times; otherwise crew-operated with a BW (Watermate) key. The chamber has three sets of gates; the bottom and middle pairs are normally used for pleasure craft. See the note on page 20 about keys and advice for crew operation of the large powered locks.

Pump-Out
At lock, see note re card operation, page 21.

Walking
There are pleasant walks between the town and Long Sandall Lock, where the path is along the top of the floodbank between the river and the navigation. However, direct access is difficult with overgrown towpaths at Doncaster and an obscured path near Long Sandall Lock.

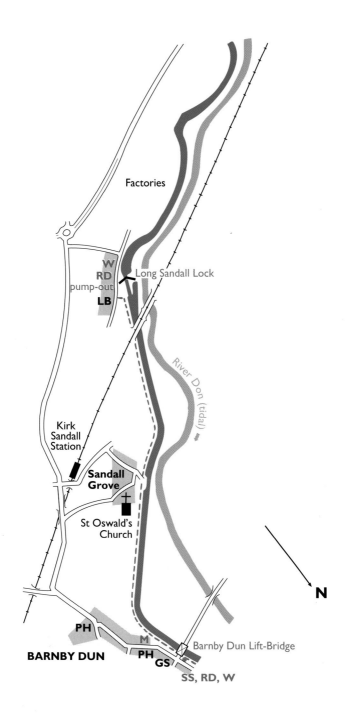

Factories

W
RD
pump-out
LB

Long Sandall Lock

River Don (tidal)

Kirk
Sandall
Station

Sandall
Grove

St Oswald's
Church

N

PH

BARNBY DUN

M
PH
GS

Barnby Dun Lift-Bridge

SS, RD, W

Three views of the the award-winning Long Sandall Lock

St Oswald's Church alongside the waterway

Map 8: *Don Navigation, New Junction Canal, Stainforth & Keadby Canal*

Barnby Dun – Kirkhouse Green – Stainforth

3.5 miles

General Area

The floodbank for the tidal River Don is never far away, usually covered in neatly-mown grass. Throughout the centuries, flooding of the lowlands here has been a problem and it was not really controlled until the 1950s. Bramwith Junction marks a change in landscape — the Don Navigation is enclosed, but the other two canals go through open and remote countryside. The Stainforth & Keadby Canal is accompanied by quiet countryside, only skirting the edge of Stainforth. On the New Junction Canal the surroundings are agricultural with farms and cottages in a pleasant, ordered landscape.

Thorpe Marsh Power Station

Due to be demolished in 1995. If you cannot see it — it has been!

Bramwith Lock

Keels going upstream left their coggy boats (dinghies) here, paying a 6d fee to the keeper and collecting them on the way back. The lock was lengthened in 1932 with three sets of gates to allow Tom Puddings (see page 12) to go from Hatfield Colliery to the power stations at Thorpe Marsh and Ferrybridge.

Flooding

Before the 1940s the land between Bramwith and Stainforth used to flood nearly every winter. The keel boatmen steered by trees and hedges when the canal banks were under water.

Don Aqueduct

Its guillotine gates were designed to prevent flooding between the river and the canal at exceptionally high tides. On one side there is substantial ironwork, but on the other side there is nothing to guard the drop to the river. Due to be renovated in 1995.

Dutch River

This is the name of the River Don's lower reaches because the artificial course was built in the 17th century by the Dutch engineer Cornelius Vermuyden.

Moveable Bridges

Common throughout the area on navigable waterways, they allowed the sailing keels to pass without lowering their masts. By 1845 all the bridges up to Doncaster were moveable so that trade was not delayed.

Navigation

Barnby Dun Lift-Bridge

Powered; keeper on duty at busy times; otherwise crew-operated with a BW (Watermate) key. Barriers and traffic lights work automatically. If going upstream, close the lid, and remove the BW (Watermate) key during the pause before the road barriers rise. This makes crossing the road to a boat easier than when the traffic is flowing.

Barnby Dun

Moorings are near the bridge for the newsagent and general store.

Bramwith Lock

Manual operation; standard windlass; keeper on duty at busy times. The chamber has three sets of gates; the top and middle pairs are normally used. The traffic lights are not used. Hook the ground chains onto the closed top gates as they tend to swing open.

Bramwith Swing-Bridge

Powered; fully automatic operation with a BW (Watermate) key. The nearby sanitary station has separate moorings, and includes showers (50p coins). See debit cards, page 21.

Stainforth Bridge

Blind approach from both directions.

Don Aqueduct

The guillotine gates are only lowered during tidal emergencies on the river below.

Low Lane Swing-Bridge, Top Lane Lift-Bridge and Kirkhouse Green Lift-Bridge

Powered operation including road barriers; crew-operated with a BW (Watermate) key. May be keeper-operated on busy summer weekends.

Walking

At Bramwith Lock the towpath crosses on the top gates. There are footbridges across and along the Don Aqueduct. The towpath also changes banks at Stainforth.

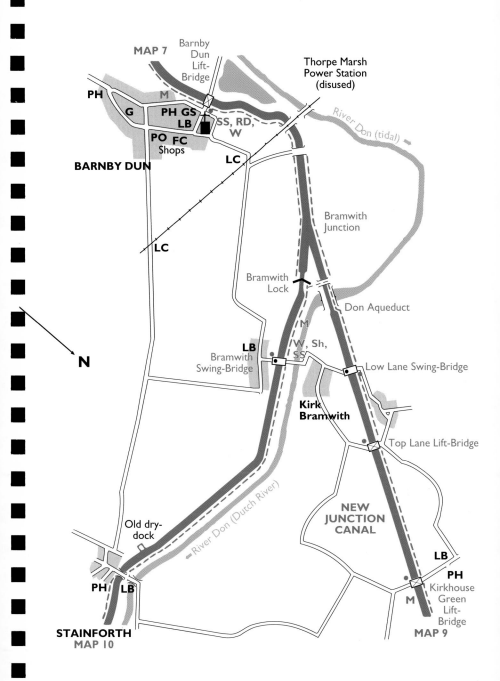

MAP 7

Barnby
Dun
Lift-
Bridge

Thorpe Marsh
Power Station
(disused)

River Don (tidal)

PH

M

G

PH GS

LB

PO FC

Shops

SS, RD,
W

BARNBY DUN

LC

LC

Bramwith
Junction

Bramwith
Lock

Don Aqueduct

M

LB

Bramwith
Swing-Bridge

W, Sh,
SS

Low Lane Swing-Bridge

Kirk
Bramwith

Top Lane Lift-Bridge

N

NEW
JUNCTION
CANAL

Old dry-
dock

River Don (Dutch River)

LB

PH

PH LB

Kirkhouse
Green
Lift-
Bridge

M

STAINFORTH
MAP 10

MAP 9

67

The New Junction Canal crosses the tidal River Don via the unique Don Aqueduct.

Bramwith Swing-Bridge

Cruising at Stainforth

Map 9: *New Junction Canal*
Kirkhouse Green – Southfield Junction
3.75 miles

General Area
A quiet landscape with no main roads and no railways. Peaceful. Views past the accompanying hedgerow are of flat fields dappled with trees. At the water's edge the vegetation reaches over the steel piling, so waterbird activity is general. Herons are often near Sykehouse Lane Lift-bridge, and in the summer swallows swoop low over the Went Aqueduct. The junction with the Aire & Calder Navigation is a remote spot with varied birdsong, wild flowers, and no traffic noise. Southfield Reservoir is a haven for wintering birds.

Thorpe Marsh Power Station
Situated near the southern end of the canal, the immense cooling towers and chimneys dominate the skyline, seen for the whole length of this straight waterway. However, the power station ceased operation in April 1994 and the towers and chimneys are due to be demolished in 1995.

Sykehouse Lock and Bridge
Built for large commercial craft, in contrast the chamber is crossed by an ancient wooden bridge that has to be swung manually.

Went Aqueduct
Carrying the canal over the River Went, this is a fabricated steel trough with concrete paved pathways on both sides. It is due to be renovated in 1995/96.

Aire & Calder Navigation
The 112-acre reservoirs at Southfield Junction serve the Aire & Calder Navigation. They compensate for the substantial loss of water in that waterway when the massive locks at Goole are used.

Navigation

Sykehouse Lock
Powered; keeper-operated at busy times. The BW (Watermate) key point is by the centre tower, not at the control boxes at each end of the chamber. If the BW (Watermate) key will not remove at the end of the sequence, it may be that the third (side) paddle on the top gates has not been closed. There is a manual swing-bridge across the centre of the large chamber. Narrowboats do not need to move the bridge when the lock is empty; large cruisers do need it cleared. When going upstream, boats with sufficient clearance can pass under the bridge to the front of the chamber and will therefore not need to move the bridge. If doing this, do not stop in the chamber under the bridge when the lock is filling, and keep back from the turbulence near the top gates.

Kirk Lane Swing-Bridge and Sykehouse Lane Lift-Bridge
Powered and fully automatic; crew-operated with a BW (Watermate) key.

Southfield Junction
Large commercial vessels use the Aire & Calder Navigation.

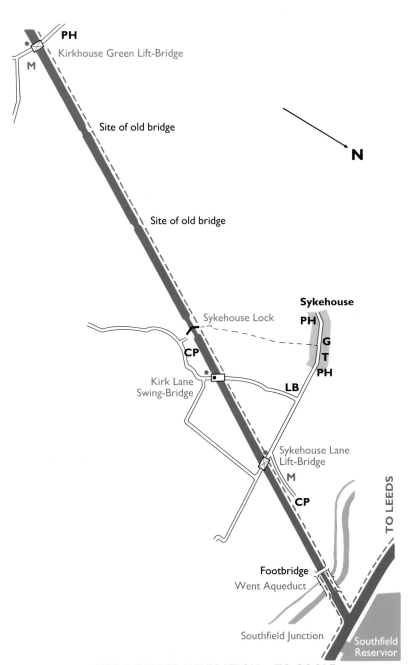

PH

Kirkhouse Green Lift-Bridge

M

Site of old bridge

Site of old bridge

N

Sykehouse

Sykehouse Lock

PH

CP

G
T

Kirk Lane
Swing-Bridge

PH

LB

Sykehouse Lane
Lift-Bridge

M

CP

TO LEEDS

Footbridge

Went Aqueduct

Southfield Junction

**Southfield
Reservior**

AIRE & CALDER NAVIGATION—-TO GOOLE

New Junction Canal

Pleasant Moorings, Kirkhouse Green

Sykehouse Lane Lift-Bridge

Went Aqueduct

Southfield Junction

Map 10: *Stainforth & Keadby Canal*
Stainforth – Thorne Railway Bridge
3.5 miles

General Area
The north bank is usually part of the tidal River Don defences — sometimes tall steel piling, otherwise a neatly-mown grassy floodbank. Between Stainforth and the M18 the canal is quiet with telegraph poles the only sign of the outside world — not a building to be seen, only trees, hedges, grass, and wild flowers. In the summer the songs of skylarks and wrens are common. Thorne is on a slight hill, an island when the flat landscape was the Trent's marshy flood-plain.

Stainforth Bridge
This used to be a swing-bridge, as did most of the fixed crossings on this canal. It allowed the old sailing keels to pass without lowering their masts.

Stainforth
Many boatmen had houses here — families helped as crew on the keels but they always had a home ashore. There is a Sunday market.

Stainforth Basin
Before the New Junction Canal and the Stainforth & Keadby Canal were built, the only outlet for boats was via the River Don to Goole, and access to the river was via a lock at the rear of this basin. When the lock closed in 1939, it ended centuries of navigation on the lower Don.

Winding Hole and Colliery Opposite
Where the Tom Puddings (see page 12) turned when calling for coal at Hatfield Colliery Wharf on the opposite bank.

Thorne Lock
When going upstream, keels left their river gear here — leeboards and anchors — and for a one-shilling fee the lock-keeper looked after them until they were collected on the return trip.

Dunston's Boatbuilders
Dunston's built a variety of vessels at Thorne, starting with wooden keels and sloops in 1858. Page 77 has more details.

Canal Tavern
There are waterway photographs in the bar. The Friday of Thorne Fair was always Water Sports Day, organised by a keelmen committee with their headquarters in this pub. Crowds of spectators gathered by the water to watch coggy-boat and barrel races, swimming events, and 'walking the greasy pole'.

Rail Bridge
Many of the vessels built at the Dunston yard were too tall to pass under the rail bridge. So the superstructures were built separately and floated down on lighters and under the bridge. Heavy lifting gear was kept in the downstream adjacent field; here the upperworks of the vessels were lifted onto the hulls and the ships completed.

Navigation

Stainforth Bridge
Blind approach from both directions.

Thorne Cruising Club and Staniland's Marina
Contact details are on page 94.

Thorne Swing-Bridge
Operation interlocked with adjacent lock; manual push open; both road barriers hand-operated. Due for renewal in 1995/96

Thorne Lock
Powered; keeper on duty at busy times; otherwise crew-operated with a BW (Watermate) key. The single control panel is confusing because it's been installed parallel to the lock chamber, instead of at right-angles to it. If you imagine it turned 90° so that your right arm is next to the chamber, all will become clear. The paddles open in timed stages when the buttons are pressed once.

Thorne
Finger moorings near the sanitary station are good for shops, market, and banks. Access to the road is via a BW (Watermate) keyed gate behind the sanitary station. Adjacent to the moorings is *Thorne Boat Services*, offering Calor, diesel, repairs and chandlery. The telephone number is on page 94.

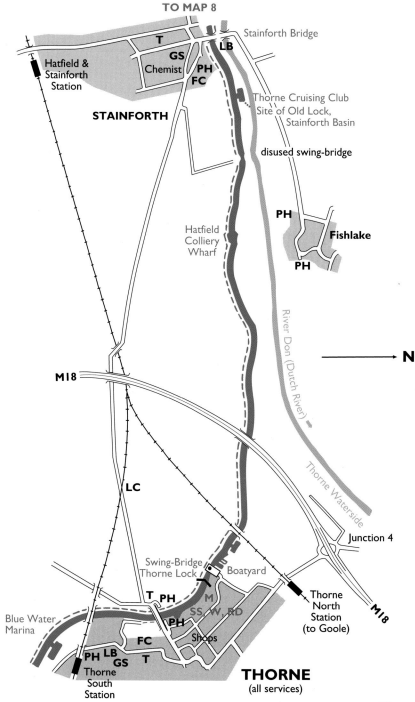

TO MAP 8

Stainforth Bridge

T

GS

Chemist

PH

FC

LB

Hatfield &
Stainforth
Station

STAINFORTH

Thorne Cruising Club
Site of Old Lock,
Stainforth Basin

disused swing-bridge

PH

Fishlake

PH

Hatfield
Colliery
Wharf

River Don (Dutch River)

N

M18

Thorne Waterside

LC

Junction 4

Swing-Bridge
Thorne Lock

Boatyard

Thorne
North
Station
(to Goole)

M18

T PH

M
SS, W, RD

PH

Shops

Blue Water
Marina

FC

PH LB
GS T

Thorne
South
Station

THORNE
(all services)

Stainforth

Lock crew 'in action', Thorne Lock

Thorne

All shops, banks, etc. can be found in Thorne. Market days are on Tuesdays, Fridays and Saturdays.

Thorne is an old market town with two distinct chapters in its waterway history. From as early as 1500 it was a port on the River Don; by 1740 it was a busy transhipment point between river and coastal vessels. Ships sailed from Thorne's Waterside area to York, Hull, London and Europe, and the busy river port had warehouses, six inns, rope- and sail-making businesses and a Customs House.

Thorne's second chapter started in 1802 when it gained another waterfront, on the new Stainforth & Keadby Canal. Eventually water traffic moved to the canal rather than the unpredictable river, and Thorne moved with it, calling the area Canalside rather than Waterside where the old river port used to be. Boats were built and maintained on the canal and many keel boatmen had a home in the town.

Now the only sign of the river port at Waterside is the John Bull pub that commemorates the *John Bull* paddle-steamer that ran a regular service from Thorne to Hull for many years. Even the river has left, diverted into a straighter course behind floodbanks.

Before the coming of the railways, Thorne was an important water–road passenger interchange. Coaches came from Doncaster and Sheffield, and canal packet-boats went to Keadby to link with the steamers on the Trent and the river steamers direct to Hull. Competition was fierce between the passenger boats on the canal and the river. In 1856 the first passenger train reached Thorne.

Boatbuilding

Thorne's river frontage was the major shipbuilding centre on the Don, and was so for many centuries. Boats up to 400 tons were built there during the late 1790s and a 24-gun warship for the Royal Navy was completed in 1804. The trade eventually drifted across to the canal where, in 1858, Richard Dunston started to build wooden vessels. By 1890 boatbuilding on the river was almost at an end, but on the canal Dunston's business thrived. After 1933 the yard built tugs for the Thames, the Admiralty and the LNER, as well as tankers, coasters, barges, lighters, fishing boats, and floating docks. In 1958, below Thorne Lock, Dunston's had nine shipbuilding berths and a dry-dock, but the yard closed in 1987 and the site has been completely cleared.

Dunston's Boatbuilders, 1981

Map 11: *Stainforth & Keadby Canal*
Thorne Railway Bridge – Medge Hall
3.5 miles

General Area

There are open views over tree-dotted fields on both sides, the A18 quiet in the distance. The canal is on the edge of Thorne Moors — the vast lands to the north that are a valuable nesting area for a wide variety of birds. In late spring the song of the nightingale may be heard; in the summer male nightjars 'churr'. Moorhens, great crested grebes, coots and herons may be seen where the reeds spill over the piling that lines both banks. See 'Wildlife' on page 25 for bird details. The wine-glass-shaped white tower provides water pressure for Thorne's domestic supplies, necessary in this low-lying landscape. On the north-west horizon the chimney with a cluster of cooling towers is Drax, the largest coal-fired power station in western Europe.

Moveable Bridges

When the working keels sailed here, each swing-bridge was usually operated by the lengthman's wife, living in an adjacent house. The boatmen signalled their approach by foghorn and she would come out and open the bridge so that the keel did not have to stop. The payment was one penny, dropped into a bag she held out on a stick — it was a long wait at the bridge on the return trip if payment was not made! Although the lengthmen's wages were low, their families usually had the benefit of a vegetable garden, a few hens and a pig or two.

Navigation

Blue Water Marina

Slipway, fuel, pump-out and chandlery. The telephone number is on page 94.

Wykewell Lift-Bridge

Powered; crew-operated with a BW (Watermate) key; fully automatic barriers and traffic lights. Carries a busy road. Instructions and controls are in a lidded box: if the lid sticks, press it down and try the BW key again.

Moore's Swing-Bridge

New bridge; powered; crew-operated with a BW (Watermate) key. Both road barriers are manually operated. Instructions and controls are in a lidded box; the BW key can only be removed when the lid is closed.

Maud's Swing-Bridge

Crew-operated; use a BW (Watermate) key to activate it, then push the beams. Both road barriers work by hand.

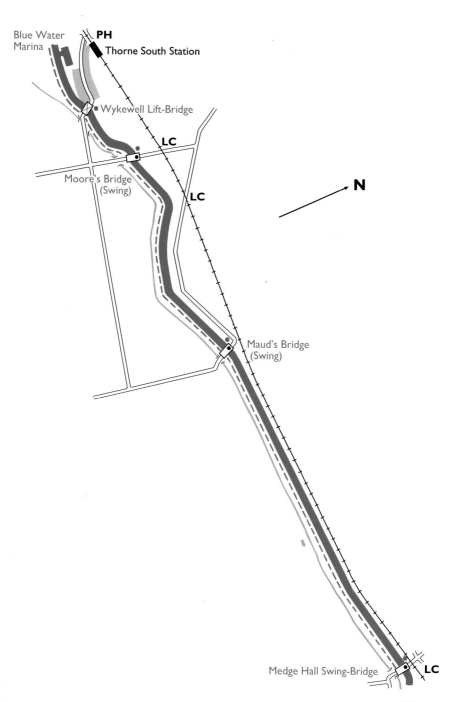

Blue Water Marina

PH

Thorne South Station

Wykewell Lift-Bridge

LC

Moore's Bridge (Swing)

LC

N

Maud's Bridge (Swing)

Medge Hall Swing-Bridge

LC

Maud's Swing-Bridge

Railway and canal at Crowle

Map 12: *Stainforth & Keadby Canal*
Medge Hall – Crowle
2.5 miles

General Area
The embanked canal gives views across hundreds of fertile acres. In the summer there are fields of blue flax, red poppies, and yellow rapeseed. It is quiet here, with more trees than further east. The old and new swing-bridges are interesting features. The railway alongside does not carry heavy traffic, the tracks often hidden by a low bank.

Kink in Canal
Between Medge Hall and Godnow bridges there is a kink in an otherwise straight canal. I do not know the reason for this, but it cannot be coincidence that it was (is) the county border between Yorkshire and Lincolnshire.

Disabled Anglers' Access, Wiseman Bridge
Over a parallel drainage ditch, it was built with funding from the NRA and BW and gives access to the towpath. There is a car park.

Crowle Wharf
There was once a swing-bridge here and the site of it can be seen on the non-towpath side. The patterned and coloured brickwork of the bridge house is attractive but the wharf buildings are almost ruins.

Navigation

Swing-Bridges

At the two swing-bridges on this section the road barrier on the far side has to be lowered manually; the near side is barred by rail staff closing level-crossing gates. BW (Watermate) keys can only be removed when the road barriers are locked back open.

Medge Hall Swing-Bridge

A new bridge, built in 1995. BW (Watermate) key; manual open.

Godnow Swing-Bridge

A modern bridge; BW (Watermate) key activates powered operation.

Walking

Towpath

Complete and generally wide, although somewhat scrubby in areas and a little uneven. In the fishing season there will be anglers and their cars on the bank for quite a distance. Confusingly, Crowle station is canal-side at Ealand, whereas Crowle is approximately a mile away. The A161 flyover is the only way across to the towpath from the station.

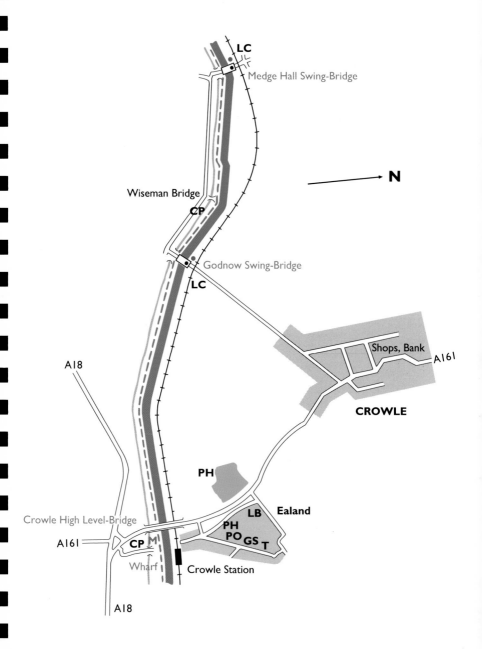

LC

Medge Hall Swing-Bridge

N

Wiseman Bridge

CP

Godnow Swing-Bridge

LC

A18

Shops, Bank

A161

CROWLE

PH

PH

LB

Ealand

PH

PO GS T

Crowle High Level-Bridge

A161

CP M

Wharf

Crowle Station

A18

Keadby Scenes

Sliding railway bridge

Narrowboat Penny

Locking out into the River Trent

Coasters on the River Trent near Keadby Lock

Map 13: *Stainforth & Keadby Canal*
Crowle – Keadby
3.5 miles

General Area
What was once the flood-plain of the River Trent is flat and agricultural with few trees. The canal is raised on an embankment with fields to the southern horizon. It can be breezy with the winds unrestricted by the flat landscape. The sky looks large. Near Crowle the land is slightly higher and rail embankments occasionally restrict the scenery. The railway along the north bank is not busy. At Keadby, shipping activity on the Trent and boating passage of the lock depends on the state of the tide on the river.

Keadby Rail Bridge
A complex web of girders and beams. Built in 1926, it opens by the span retracting into its abutment.

New Gas Power Station
Built in 1994 on the site of a previous coal-powered station, it is part of the 'dash for gas'.

Petrol Explosion
In the 1920s and 1930s most of Sheffield's petrol came to the city by boat, carried in iron tanks in otherwise ordinary wooden holds. In 1926 one such vessel, the *Two Sisters*, exploded at Keadby as her tanks were being filled. Two men were killed.

Keadby Lock
The gates are opened and closed with chains that are pulled around capstans by the lock-keeper, although if funding can be found the lock will be power-operated after 1996. There are two sets of gates at each end of the lock, making it usable even when the river tides reach a higher level than the canal.

Navigation

Vazon Swing-Bridge
Manual crew operation; a BW (Watermate) key needed to activate it.

Keadby Rail Bridge
Operated by rail staff who can see waiting boats from the signal box; some boats sound a horn. There is usually only a short delay, but sometimes it can be twenty minutes if three or four trains are due. Boats waiting on either side of the bridge cannot see each other.

Moorings
Both banks above Keadby Lock; those by the towpath have a car park alongside. Shower (50p coins); see debit card note, page 21.

Keadby Marine
Marine and general engineers; contact details are on page 94.

Keadby Swing-Bridge
Immediately above the lock; operated by the lock-keeper.

Keadby Lock
The lock is always operated by the keeper, and only at set states of the tide. Hours and entering from the river is covered on the 'Trent Navigation' section on pages 90-91.

Walking

Towpath
Complete and generally wide, although somewhat scrubby in areas and a little uneven. At weekends in the fishing season, anglers' cars are dotted along the path, especially near Keadby. *At Keadby Rail Bridge the towpath crosses the tracks — please take care.*

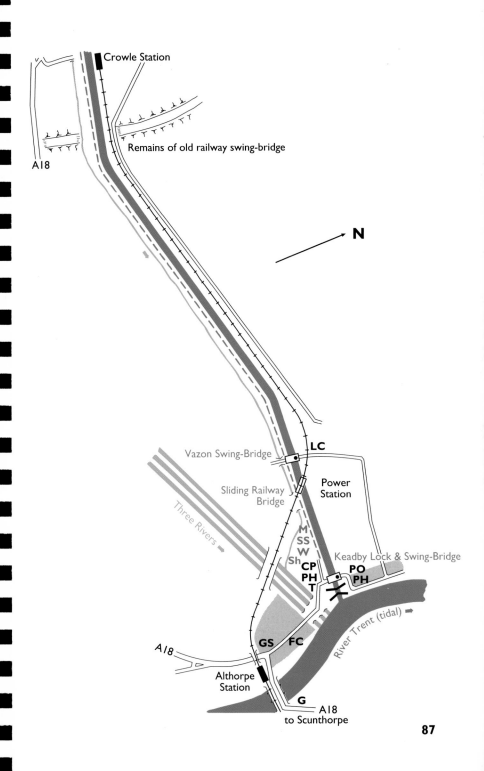

Crowle Station

Remains of old railway swing-bridge

A18

N

Vazon Swing-Bridge

LC

Power
Station

Sliding Railway
Bridge

Three Rivers

Keadby Lock & Swing-Bridge

M
SS
W
Sh
CP
PH
T

PO
PH

River Trent (tidal)

GS   FC

A18

Althorpe
Station

G   A18
to Scunthorpe

The manual chain and windlass operation of Keadby lock-gates may soon be superseded.

Entrance to Keadby Lock from the River Trent

Navigating the River Trent

The Trent at Keadby is tidal and carries large commercial vessels, some of which call at the wharfs either side of the lock entrance. However, do not allow these facts to deter you: to be safe you must respect the Trent, not fear it. Many small boats — cruisers and narrowboats — use the tidal Trent to reach various canals. Ask — and follow — the advice given by BW at Cromwell Lock. Also helpful is an item by John Lower in the July 1988 edition of *Waterways World* magazine: 'Calculated Cruising: Trent Tideway Tips'.

Navigating the Trent

Before setting out, check your boat and its equipment and ensure you have adequate fuel. Boat ropes should be at least 30 feet long to enable them to reach the locksides. Carry an anchor and cable (minimum 60 feet), free of obstructions and ready to drop. Many boat crews wear life jackets and this is strongly recommended, especially for children. Use the tide to help your journey: fighting it is a waste of fuel and time. River charts are recommended (see opposite page).

Remember that large vessels need the deep channel: try to meet them on a straight section, move over to one side, and *stay* there. Do not dart about undecided. They may use horn signals and will appreciate it if you know what they mean. Keep a good lookout fore and aft and concentrate. The large vessels travel fast, but if you see them and move out of the way there should be no problems.

Aegre (Pronounced 'ā-ger')

The Aegre is a tidal bore which occasionally travels up the river from the Humber to Torksey or beyond. The National Rivers Authority issues a free annual timetable (see opposite page). The wave may be a few inches to five feet in height and it occurs at Flood. It usually needs a tide of over 8.5 metres at Hull, no flood water in the river, and no wind. However, if you cannot avoid it, meet it head-on in the middle of the river.

Keadby Lock

The lock can only operate when the tide is high enough to give clearance over the entrance. See opposite page for hours of operation. The bottom gates open direct from the Trent and are kept closed unless the keeper knows you are coming.

If you arrive too early or late, or the gates are shut, there is a holding berth approximately 150 yards downstream of the lock. Boats on the holding berth are not to be left unattended; no mooring overnight is allowed, and craft must move if asked to do so by Keadby Generation personnel. Commercial craft use the quay 6–7 times a year and they have priority. Latest information is available from BW's Doncaster office (see page 94).

The position of Keadby Lock entrance is as shown on page 89. *Always turn into the flow to approach the lock entrance or the holding berth.*

River Trent Navigation Facts

Definition of Terms

Ebb Tide: when the river is running out towards the sea.

Flood: when the tide stops ebbing and turns to come back in; it changes direction very quickly.

Flood Tide: when the tide is running in; lasts approximately 3 hours; the flow is very fast.

High Water: the tide stops running in.

Slack Water: the tide is not going in or out; lasts approximately ten minutes. Then the Ebb Tide starts.

Spring Tides: Twice a month; tides that rise to the highest High Water levels.

Neap Tides: Twice a month; the tides that only reach the lowest High Water levels.

Tide Tables and Aegre Schedule

National Rivers Authority, Corringham Road, Gainsborough DN21 1QH. Tel: 01427 612205. Tide tables £2 in 1995. Aegre schedule free.

Tide Tables are also available from British Waterways' area office at Newark (see page 94) and most tidal locks. Price: £1.

Trent Charts

Trent (Tidal), *Trent (Non-Tidal)* and *The Yorkshire Ouse*. All three charts are available from: The Trent Boating Association, 78 Old Retford Road, Sheffield S13 9RA. £4.50 each, post paid. Also available at Cromwell Lock.

Keadby Lock

Phone the lock to book passage. Please try to give at least 24 hours' notice as congestion may prevent passage on some days, especially summer weekends.

Maximum Size of Craft: 77ft × 21ft.

Radio Frequency: Calling channel 16; working channel 74. The radio is *not* constantly manned.

Operating Hours: Currently:
  May–September: Mon–Fri 06.00–22.00; Sat–Sun 06.00–20.00 inc. 2 × 30min. breaks dependent on tides.
  Winter: Mon–Thur 08.00–16.30; Fri 08.00–15.30.

Trent Locks Telephones

Keadby	01724 782205
West Stockwith	01427 890204
Torksey	01428 771202
Cromwell	01636 821213

Licences

The Trent here is controlled by Associated British Ports, but a standard canal licence does cover use of the river to reach the SSYN. If you do not have a British Waterways canal licence, then a temporary haven licence is required to use Keadby Lock, or a short-stay canal licence. All are available from the Keadby lock-keeper.

Moorings

Temporary moorings can be arranged with the lock-keeper, but long stays should be booked prior to arrival.

Horn Signals

1 blast	I am turning to starboard (right)
2 blasts	I am turning to port (left)
3 blasts	My engines are going in reverse

Public Houses

Map	Location	Distance from canal (yards)	Pub Name	Telephone	Meals	Children	Beer Garden	B + B
1	Worksop Road Aqueduct	100	The Fox House	0114 244 2366	L			✔
1	Worksop Road Aqueduct	50	The Cocked Hat	0114 244 8332	L		✔	
1	Tinsley Lock, No. 8		The Plumpers	0114 244 1457				
2	Rotherham Town Lock	100	The Phoenix	01709 364611	L E	✔		✔
2	Rotherham Town Lock	200	The Bridge	01709 363683	L	✔		
2	Greasbrough Road Bridge	†	Crinoline Bridge Inn	01709 370748	L			
3/4	Kilnhurst Moorings		The Commercial	01709 587905		✔		
3/4	Kilnhurst Moorings		The Ship Inn	01709 584322	L E	✔	✔	
4	Swinton Sanitary Stn	200	The Ship	01709 582227				
4	Swinton Sanitary Stn	200	The Red House	01709 583242				
4	Mexborough Top Lock	100	The Ferry Boat	01709 586382		✔	✔	
4	Mexborough Top Lock	150	The George & Dragon	01709 584375			✔	
4	Mexborough Top Lock	250	New Mason's Arms	01709 583439	L	✔	✔	
4	Pastures Bridge Moorings	150	The Miner's Arms	01709 583547				
5	Sprotbrough		The Boat Inn	01302 857188	L E	M	✔	
5	Sprotbrough Village	800	Ivanhoe	01302 853130	✔	✔	✔	
7/8	Barnby Dun	350	The Star	01302 882571	L E	M	✔	✔
10	Stainforth		New Inn	01302 841614	L E	✔	✔	
10	Thorne Moorings	50	Canal Tavern	01405 813688	L E	M	✔	
10	Thorne Moorings	150	Rising Sun	01405 812688		✔	✔	
11	Wykewell Br/Blue Water Marina	300	Victoria	01405 813163	L E	M	✔	
12/13	Crowle Bridge/Ealand	400	New Trent Inn	01724 710315	L E	M		
13	Keadby Lock		The Friendly Fox	01724 782243	L E	✔	✔	
13	Keadby Lock	50	The Old South Yorkshire	01724 783518	L E	✔		
New Junction Canal								
8/9	Kirkhouse Green Bridge	300	The Hacienda	01405 785648	‡	‡	‡	‡
9	Sykehouse Lane Bridge	1200	The Three Horseshoes	01405 785273		✔	✔	
9	Sykehouse Lane Bridge	1300	The Old George	01405 785635	L E	✔	✔	

† Accessible when towpath improvements are completed.

‡ Closed at the time of writing.

Key — Meals: **L** = Lunchtime; **E** = Evenings. Children: ✔ = Children welcome;
M = Children welcome when taking a meal

N.B. Facilities provided by pubs are liable to change — it is recommended to phone in advance.

Public Transport

Rail

Sheffield and Rotherham, Tel: 0114 272 6411. Doncaster: 01302 340222.

Stations near the SSYN are on the Sheffield–Rotherham–Mexborough–Conisbrough–Doncaster line. It may be necessary to change at Doncaster for Stainforth, Thorne South, Crowle, Althorpe (Keadby).

Note: Crowle station is at Ealand by the canal, not at Crowle.

Buses

Sheffield, Rotherham, Doncaster areas: SYPTE, Tel: 0114 276 8688. Doncaster Busline: 01302 344949

Sheffield Supertram

Map 1 shows the route near the canal, and includes the city centre and Meadowhall shopping centre. Other branches go to all parts of Sheffield, every 10 minutes, 7 days a week.

Information Line: 0114 276 8688. The three canal-side stops with towpath access are Attercliffe, Arena/Don Valley Stadium and Carbrook. All stops have blue/grey ticket machines; coins £1, 50p, 20p, 10p, 5p. A single trip is £1 per adult; within one fare-stage is 50p. *Tickets must be time- and date-stamped in the yellow machines before boarding.*

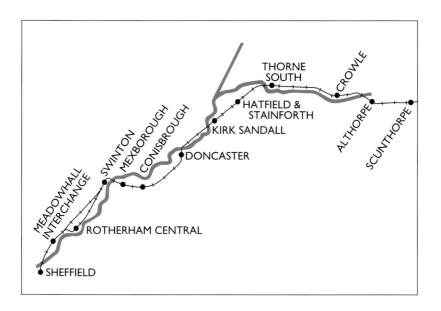

93

Further Information

Telephone Numbers

British Waterways

Doncaster Office	01302 340610
Keadby Lock	01724 782205
Tinsley Locks	0114 244 1579
	or 0114 244 1981
Sheffield Basin Master	0114 272 2003
Waterways Manager (Newark)	01636 704481

Inland Waterways Association

1 Vicarage Way, Arksey, Doncaster DN5 0TG.
01302 873127

National Rivers Authority

Rivers House, 21 Park Square South, Leeds
LS1 2QG. 0113 2440191

Tourist Information

Doncaster	01302 734309
Rotherham	01709 823611
Sheffield	0114 273 4671
	and 0114 279 5901

Meadowhall shopping complex	0114 256 9999
Doncaster Countryside Service	01302 737411
Conisbrough Castle	01709 863329
Sprotbrough Flash	01904 659570
Sheila Bury, Waterway Artist	01302 856902

Sports Facilities in Sheffield near the Canal

Ponds Forge International Sports Centre
(swimming and diving), near the canal basin
	0114 279 9766
Don Valley Stadium	0114 256 0607
Sheffield Arena	0114 256 5500

Boatyards/Marinas

Sheffield Canal Company, Victoria Boatyard,
Sheffield. 0114 272 7233

Tulley's Marine Services, Northfield Road,
Rotherham. 01709 836743

E.V. Waddington, The Boatyard, Swinton,
Mexborough S64 8AT. 01709 582232

Yorkshire Rose Marina, Unit 9, Leach Lane,
Mexborough S64 0EN. 01709 571555

Stanilands & Co. Ltd, Thorne, Doncaster
DN8 5ES. 01405 813150

Thorne Boat Services, Orchard Street, Thorne,
Doncaster. 01405 814197

Blue Water Marina, Southend, Thorne,
Doncaster DN8 5QR. 01405 813165

Keadby Marine Ltd, Canal Side, Keadby, South
Humberside DN17 3ED. 01724 782302

Trip-Boats

Alan Oliver Cruises, Tall Pines, Cadeby Road,
Sprotbrough, Doncaster DN5 7SD.
01302 856513

Ashanti Gold. Based at Stanley Ferry.
Party bookings. 0860 866843

Sheffield Canal Company: see opposite.

Community and Group Venture Boats

Sobriety and *Eden.* The Sobriety Centre, Dutch
River Side, Goole DN14 5TB. 01405 768730

Spider. John Turberville, Dinnington Youth &
Community Centre, Doe Quarry Lane,
Dinnington, Sheffield S31 7NH. 01909 550577

Hire-Boats

Yorkshire Rose Marina, Mexborough: see
above.

Banks Hire Boats, Selby. 01347 821772

Shire Cruisers, Sowerby Bridge. 01422 832712

Boat Clubs

Strawberry Island Boat Club, Milethorne Lane,
Doncaster. 01302 364954

Thorne Cruising Club, 2 North Street, Thorne,
South Humberside DN17 3JN. 01302 734194

Angling Clubs/Societies

See angling section, page 19

Maps

Ordnance Survey; Landranger Series, maps
111, 112.

Further Reading

Fletcher, Harry, *A Life on the Humber* (Faber &
Faber, 1975; ISBN 0-571-10723-0).
Memories of sailing keels on the SSYN.

Taylor, Mike, *Memories of the Sheffield & South
Yorkshire Navigation* (Yorkshire Waterway
Publications, 1988). Pictorial history of the
SSYN.

Other Waterway Guides of the Area.

Richardson, Christine, and John Lower, *A
Walkers' and Boaters' Guide to the
Chesterfield Canal and Cuckoo Way*
(Sheffield: The Hallamshire Press, 1994;
ISBN 1-874718-25-3). Another in the
'Richlow' series of guides.

Calder Navigation Society, *West Yorkshire
Waterway Guide*
(1992; ISBN 0-9512400-1-3).

Index

Also available from The Hallamshire Press

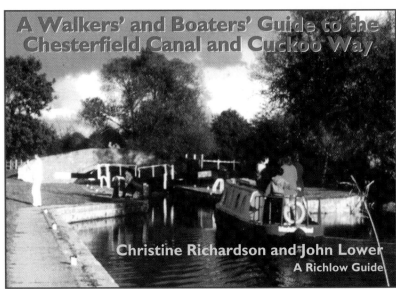

A Walkers' and Boaters' Guide to the Chesterfield Canal and Cuckoo Way

Christine Richardson and John Lower

A Richlow Guide

£5.95

ISBN 1 874718 25 3